T0146564

The
Humpty Dumpty Principle

The Great Fall
Brings A Dark Night

Don't Wait For All The King's Horses
And All The King's Men

You Can Put Yourself
Together Again

Cycle Journey Series:
Book One

Court Johnson and Sylvia Stallings

BALBOA.
PRESS

A DIVISION OF HAY HOUSE

Balboa Press books may be ordered through booksellers or by contacting:

Balboa Press
A Division of Hay House
1663 Liberty Drive
Bloomington, IN 47403
www.balboapress.com
1 (877) 407-4847

Print information available on the last page.

ISBN: 978-1-5043-4425-8 (sc)
ISBN: 978-1-5043-4457-9 (hc)
ISBN: 978-1-5043-4456-2 (e)

Library of Congress Control Number: 2015919622

Balboa Press rev. date: 1/8/2016

The Cycle Journey Series

Four Books That Explore Your Life Path

The Humpty Dumpty Principle
The Great Fall Brings A Dark Night
You Can Put Yourself Together Again

The Golden Thought
The Quest To Lead An Extraordinary Life
Live Your Dreams

A New You
The Art Of Personal Transformation

Drifting To Find Direction
Order Out Of Confusion

www.cyclejourneywisdom.com

<u>The Original Nursery Rhyme</u>

Humpty Dumpty sat on a wall,
Humpty Dumpty had a great fall,
All the king's horses and all the king's men,
Couldn't put Humpty together again.

The question that needs to be asked and answered is:
If they can't who will?

The Answer Is:

The Humpty Dumpty
PRINCIPLE

The Great Fall
Brings A Dark Night

Don't Wait For
All The King's Horses
And All The King's Men

You Can Put Yourself
Together Again

Contents

The Knowledge Base

The Humpty Dumpty Principle uses a Dark Night and a Cycle Journey as change and growth symbols. To put them to full use you will need a knowledge base of essays that incorporates key psychological topics.

C. G. Jung's Deeper Insights

- **pp12: Deeper Insight 1 – Unconscious Power**
  All that is not in the conscious and what doesn't ordinarily enter awareness.

- **pp50: Deeper Insight 2 – Your Shadow**

  This is where you store the thoughts you have repressed.

- **pp81: Deeper Insight 3 – The Self**
  The Self encompasses the entire psyche and its possibilities, including the conscious and unconscious.

- **pp110: Deeper Insight 4 – Active Imagination**
  Active imagination taps into creative potential by creating a bridge between the conscious and the unconscious.

- **pp139: Deeper Insight 5 – Individuation**
  Individuation is the gradual integration and merger of the Self through resolving successive layers of inner conflict.

- **pp174: Deeper Insight 6 – The Ego**

  It is the organizer of thoughts and intuitions, feelings, and sensations and has access to memories which are not repressed.

- **p 201: Deeper Insight 7 – The Persona**

  The persona is the face we show the world, the character we play in life and how we relate to others.

Acknowledgments

We want to acknowledge all the people who contributed ideas and encouragement to the Humpty Dumpty Principle. There were too many times to mention when we felt stuck and on the edge of giving up. Without fail someone came along with inspiration or information.

A special thank you to Doctor Lionel Corbett for his support, encouragement, and wealth of knowledge. We would also like to express our gratitude to the members of The Dream Group for their unwavering belief we could take on this challenging subject.

To June Laula, whose review and corrections are a vital part of this book, a heartfelt recognition for your eagle eye. Personal pride in our granddaughters, Kendall for her support and for taking our publicity photos and Kristi for her enthusiasm about our writing.

A well earned note of credit to the University of Metaphysical Sciences where much of the foundation for Sylvia's ideas were developed. Appreciation to Pacifica Graduate Institute where we were exposed to many of the Jungian concepts which contributed to the formation of this book and to the University of Philosophical Research where Sylvia continues her studies.

Finally, there are the Dark Night sufferers. Without their stories and the books and movies about their trials, there would be no book. The more we wrote, the more we realized the responsibility we'd taken on and the importance of doing justice to their stories.

Forward

A failed relationship, the loss of a home or job, a series of accidents or a debilitating illness, and other upheavals bring on a collapse of life's traditional meaning. What do you do? How can you move forward? The Humpty Dumpty Principle reveals how a Cycle Journey Story can create new meaning in your life.

To get you off to a quick start, we'll explain **how the book is organized.** The Cycle Journey Story describes the author's qualifications to write the Humpty Dumpty Principle and explains the value of a Cycle Journey Story. The body of the book, the presentation of each of the Cycle Journey's eight stages, begins with a short introduction. Next, in **The Essentials** section the cycle stage is defined and book and movie examples show that stage exists as part of our culture. Then there is the **Stories** section. We begin by telling Humpty's tale. In stage one the famous egg's story starts with The Tale of the Great Fall, which depicts Humpty as an every person symbol for the journey away from a great fall and the Dark Night it brings. The way we phrase it is:

The great fall is a metaphor for a Dark Night.
Humpty Dumpty has always been the symbol of the great fall.
His journey is our journey and his story is a model for our story.

Humpty's tale is followed by our Cycle Journey scenes. They serve as can do examples for our readers when they begin their own Cycle Journey Story. Along with our scenes at the end of each stage there is **Tell * Journal * Write section** full of coaching advice on how to craft your own Cycle Journey Story.

Finally, how is the Humpty Dumpty Principle meant to be used? There are two approaches. Read the book. Learn about the Cycle Journey and pay attention to the Deeper Insight essays on the work of the Swiss psychologist C. G. Jung. Go further and make full use of the book by telling, journaling, and writing eight individual scenes that when stitched together, become the Cycle Journey Story of how you moved beyond the great fall and its Dark Night.

A Special Word About Humpty Dumpty

Humpty Dumpty is a fragile, self-contained elliptical egg. His Great Fall and resulting damage signal the need for deep personal change. After his Terrible Tumble and resulting cracks and missing pieces, he is in a self-reflective state that opens up the possibility of transformation, rebirth, and becoming a golden egg.

Humpty Dumpty evokes unconscious energies that move in a spiral-like journey, at each Cycle Journey stage bringing vital new insights to light. As an egg, he symbolizes the creative fire-point within each of us, the ability to change from within. His development illustrates the magic and mystery of the transformational experience. His movement through the Cycle Journey represents the possibility of our unification of the conscious and unconscious and the creation of an individualized Self, a true golden egg.

Humpty Dumpty appeared in his present form as an 1870's English nursery rhyme. In 1902 he showed up in William Wallace Denslow's Mother Goose story book as an egg. The Humpty Dumpty name has been linked to different theories, among them that he represents the humpbacked Richard the III, and another that the name came from a large cannon that protected the English town of Colchester. His increased popularity can be traced to an appearance in Lewis Carroll's *Through the Looking Glass.*

Illustrations from the turn of the twentieth century by artists Sir John Tenniel and Blanche McManus show Humpty on a wall or on the ground after his fall. The renowned egg given human characteristics symbolized a fall from grace, a loss of status, respect or prestige, in other words the great fall. That life changing upheaval, as it does in this allegory, allows Humpty to be viewed as a symbol for a human's great fall that begins a cycle journey.

Cycle Journey Story

The Humpty Dumpty Principle is based on what has for centuries been called a Dark Night, a universal, turmoil-filled, experience that is a personal low point for almost everyone. This upheaval provides the motivation to undertake a journey to find a new and deeper meaning for existence. That search for deep change becomes a circular trip through a series of growth stages which act as the center point for your Cycle Journey Story.

As authors our view of the need for a Cycle Journey Story is personal. We have gone through our own Dark Nights, challenging and difficult times we didn't know how to get past. To discover who we are and who we were meant to be, we used our own stories as a means for Self-discovery and Self-inquiry.

First we revealed our stories to each other and journaled about what we heard. Then we used our journals to develop scenes that retold key incidents in our lives. Our purpose in the Humpty Dumpty Principle is to share our discovery of the Cycle Journey Story as a powerful pathway to change.

We want our stories to serve as proof you are not alone and we are fellow survivors who've lived through the great falls, our own terrible tumbles. Our narratives led us to see transformation involves letting go of the lives we'd planned and beginning quests for very different ones, which patiently waited for us to discover their existence. What we learned, along with the way we saw how a Cycle Journey Story could serve as a vehicle for profound change, became our inspiration and guide for this book.

Once our great falls, upheavals and resulting Dark Nights took hold, we thought the damage couldn't be undone. In the language of the Humpty Dumpty Principle we believed not even all the king's horses and all the king's men could put us together again. Our stories tell of passing through troubled and chaotic times. There were betrayals, traumas, and multiple calamities that created earthquake-like instabilities. At the deepest level we suffered heartbreak, pain, and loss.

Like Humpty and possibly like you, we realized great falls left us cracked and fractured in so many places we couldn't think clearly and were barely able to meet the demands of our daily lives. We saw life through the bleak eyes of deeply wounded victims. Our thoughts were scrambled. We felt our willpower would never be strong enough to escape our Dark Nights. Given the tumultuous nature of the time in our own wilderness, we understood our post-fall survival depended on discovering a new way to view our place in the world.

Out of a combination of determination, expanded awareness, and deeper insights, we told each other about our great falls.

To remember the repressed memories that came out of our unconscious, we kept journals. Then, when it seemed we had a firm grasp on our stories, we wrote about our falls. Those tales led to a new way to view our lives. Each time we revised and read aloud we gained a richer understanding of the forces behind our own journeys. What astounded us is how telling, journaling, and writing our stories allowed us to see common patterns which led to define an eight stage Cycle Journey. This circular evolution moved us past our great falls and Dark Nights, and plotted the course for a new direction for our lives. We recognized, backed by figurative language skills like metaphors and symbols that build a bridge into the unconscious, any person could have the same awakening.

You can **Tell * Journal * Write** your own personal story in a way that gives the same direction, depth, and focus to your life. Whether it's as an oral storyteller, in a Cycle Journey Story Journal, through the combination of written scenes, or in a mini-memoir form, you can bring new meaning and understanding to your life.

Our cycle is based on the theories of the Swiss psychologist C. G. Jung. Many of his conclusions lay a foundation for bringing feelings and emotions out of the unconscious, the part of life that does not ordinarily enter your awareness, but impacts your behavior and perception of the world.

A Dark Night brings with it challenges that may require outside help. Seek a qualified professional to discuss personal issues and life disruptions such as co-dependency, depression, prolonged grief and/or anger, mental health issues, addictions and substance abuse, and mental and/or physical abuse or destructive behavior.

The Humpty Dumpty Principle is a resource, not a substitute for therapeutic, medical, legal, financial, or other professional advice.

The Cycle Journey

The Humpty Dumpty Principle presents a Cycle Journey of change and transformation. Whether they recognize it or not, at some time in their life everyone is pulled into this cycle.

The Cycle

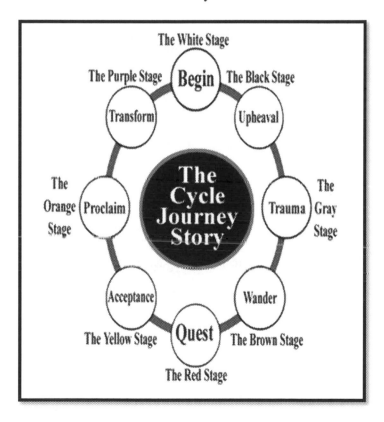

The Cycle Journey's eight stages:

1. It's **beginning, the white stage,** lies in powerful youthful commands and rules which carry into an adult's life.
2. These injunctions influence the reaction to the turmoil-filled, earthquake-like **black stage, an upheaval**.
3. **Trauma, the gray third stage**, is a struggle to find a voice for the upheaval's inner pain.
4. **Wandering, the brown stage four,** turns the Dark Night traveler toward a dazed and confused time in the wilderness.
5. **The action-oriented red stage five, the quest,** presents the possibility of growth with its search for a true destiny.
6. **In the yellow stage six, acceptance,** there's time for contemplation essential for **recognition** of the quest's results.
7. **Orange stage seven, proclaiming,** takes those deeper insights and expanded awareness into the world.
8. **At purple stage eight, transforming**, with the quest, acceptance, and proclaiming complete the ingredients for true change, a transformation are present.

The cycle is fluid. Stages are not meant to be moved through in a rigid order. You'll move back and forth between stages as you adapt to new situations, different input, and unexpected demands. No one's journey will be exactly the same. For some individual stages will be short and for others years will go by before they move on.

Two stages, like upheaval and trauma or acceptance and proclaiming can operate at the same time. Many travelers recycle as they move back and forth in the stages.

ONE

The White Stage, Begin

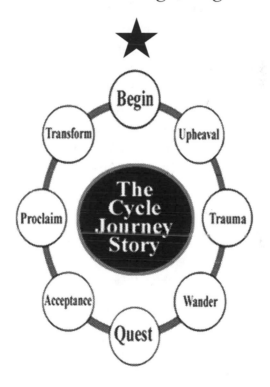

See Your Life as an Adventure
"We must let go of the life we have planned.
So as to accept the one that is waiting for us."
~Joseph Campbell, Author, Philosopher

An Introduction To Stage One

It started before it started. That contradiction makes sense when you think of the beginning as the backstory for your journey, a prelude that lays the foundation for how you'll tell about your journey in the rest of the stages. It's there to establish what came before the main part of your Cycle Journey Story.

In the Essentials we'll define the beginning stage and give examples like Jane Eyre, Batman, and Mexican artist Frida Kahlo to show how it exists in our culture. Once you have an understanding of the beginning stage you'll get a Deeper Insight into the unconscious, the psychological topic you'll work with in the stage. Then it's story time. We'll introduce you to Humpty Dumpty and start our stories by going back into childhood events that deeply influenced us as adults.

Stage One ends with Tell * Journal * Write where you'll get coaching on how to use a Cycle Journey Story Journal, and how to develop a core sentence for your beginning scene.

The Essentials

Look back. Recall childhood memories and the commands or decrees imposed by mom, dad, teachers and friends. Some, like look both ways before you cross the street or wash your hands before you eat, served as guidelines for getting along in the world. Others, such as you are smart and there's nothing you can't do or you have special talents and gifts, shaped your achievements. A few, you fail at everything you try or the reason you don't do well at school is you're lazy, turned into darker, weighty reprimands carried into adulthood.

The white stage, the beginning, looks at how the past affects the present. It targets where the Dark Night has its roots. This initial phase of the cycle examines the controlling beliefs adults often unknowingly take on in childhood and continue to employ to deal with turmoil and disorder. While positive reinforcements may have opened exciting life paths, admonishments and putdowns could have acquired unchallengeable power. They've grown into the desires and biases held in your unconscious and its shadow, the place where you keep the parts of your personality which conflict with your adult life. Those unconscious memories aren't evil or bad. They are parts of you incompatible with the conscious image you've chosen to present to the world.

The repression of childhood memories can point to present strategies for coping with a Dark Night. These approaches have their origin in a lack of self-knowledge about limiting expectations of a teacher, parent or close friend. An angry reaction to criticism could have its roots in a long ago bullying schoolmate. Early scolding, pushed into the unconscious might create a belief change is impossible and struggling against a Dark Night is useless. The adult, unaware of the limiting power of unconscious memories, has an unexplainable feeling of guilt. The great fall is viewed as simply what he or she deserves. Without a viewpoint shift, these restrictive emotions formed in childhood create roadblocks which hold you back from moving beyond an upheaval and its Dark Night.

Youthful commands can be crippling or essential survival mechanisms. For one person a failed relationship could be a relief, a job loss an opportunity and an illness a challenge. Someone else, with childhood prohibitions, sees these events as uncontrollable disasters that form the core of a Dark Night. They become virtual prisoners of their own repressed youthful fears. Those childhood dictates, often unrecognized until the appearance of the Dark Night, have grown into unyielding admonitions. To move past a Humpty Dumpty-like great fall, it's necessary to bring childhood and youthful rules and injunctions out of the unconscious and into the light of the conscious mind.

Charlotte Bronte's Jane Eyre shows how beginning directives influence the rest of life. The novel opens with ten year old orphan Jane living with her aunt's family, the Reeds. After horrible abuse Jane rises up and tells her cousins what she thinks of them. They send her to a bleak boarding school, Lowood Institute. In this friendless place Jane adopts a lifelong internal dictate that she will care for and respect herself. She states the childhood lesson this way, "I care for myself. The more solitary, the more friendless, the more unsustained I am, the more I will respect myself." This moral guide serves her well as her life moves through a series of Dark Nights and she experiences more than her share of great falls.

It may seem strange that the graphic novel **Batman** follows Jane Eyre. Bruce Wayne's tale is an example of how the beginning impacts a Dark Night. Batman is a mythic tale of how the full impact of a traumatic youthful event is repressed and stays locked in the shadow. Bruce's parents were murdered before his eyes. His admonition he would avenge their deaths by personally bringing the worst criminals to justice became a consuming unconscious dictate he could never escape.

Frida Kahlo, a great twentieth century artist, is a contrasting example of the power of youthful directives. She grew up in the early part of the twentieth century in the socialist revolutionary culture of Mexico, with a father who was a photographer. Frida developed her outsider, artistic outlook early in her life. That self-reliant view, which stayed in her unconscious, helped her to move past a near-death bus accident, which left her with wounds, including a crushed and dislocated right foot that plagued her during the rest of her life. Her independence made it easier, when she could no longer follow her dream of being a doctor, to turn to art. She stated her childhood lesson when she said, "Feet, what do I need you for when I have wings to fly."

Jane Eyre's feelings about her childhood strengthened her character. Bruce Wayne's repressed rage created Batman, a crime fighter held prisoner by the dark memories and isolated from the rest of the world. Frida Kahlo's ability to adapt shows how a transformation is aided by childhood memories brought into consciousness.

After the shock of his great fall, Humpty unexpectedly recalls conflicts with his father and a confrontation with his teacher, Mr. Poached. For him to have the insight needed to undertake his Cycle Journey, these childhood figures and their dictates need to be brought into Humpty's consciousness.

We've been surprised at the power of youthful suppressed decrees and injunctions and have learned we needed to retrieve them from our unconscious to undertake a Cycle Journey. To help bring these long repressed thoughts into the light, we used our stories as a way to build a bridge between our consciousness and memories stored in our unconscious and its shadow.

Once we'd pulled those experiences into our consciousness, our decisions started to be based on present realities not worn out childhood experiences and limitations. At the end of the Cycle Journey, we looked back and realized that our view of the childhood scenes needed to be looked at in a new way. That decision became our first step in individuation and in moving toward wholeness and balance.

Stage 1 Deeper Insight Unconscious Power

"Man's task is to become conscious of the contents that press upward from the unconscious." ~ C. G. Jung

The unconscious, the key to fully recalling childhood memories, is all that is not in the conscious. It's the part of life not ordinarily entering individual awareness, but impacts behavior and our world perception.

It can be divided into the personal unconscious, distressing and unimportant memories and painful personality parts which have not come into consciousness, and the collective unconscious, the blueprint for life within us when we are born.

In the first four stages, starting with the beginning, the emphasis is on retrieving memories relegated to the unconscious. The beginning stage, our childhood, when recalled often explains reactions to upheaval, a difficulty in expressing inner pain and a failure to escape wandering.

Court's first scene pulled memories of his father out of his unconscious and helped him see how this difficult relationship ruled his adult life and the way he reacted to his divorce. He had to work on this scene for three weeks before his unconscious released the detailed memories.

In scene one Sylvia's unconscious let go of its memories in bits and pieces. It took weeks before she could recall the details of leaving her grandparents and Court finally recalled his father's Camel cigarettes, how they smelled, and the way the pack looked and how his father smoked them at the dinner table.

The collective unconscious had an even more profound effect in the cycle's acceptance stage. Court, after writing his scenes, understood his artistic expression need came from his Irish heritage and understood the more he wrote the more he felt compelled to write. It seemed like some ancient creative impulse had been activated and he needed to come to terms with how writing created wholeness in his life.

Court and Sylvia, as they developed scenes, learned the depth of the collective unconscious is beyond imagination and contains deep drives difficult not to follow. They realized even a part of their personal unconsciousness, like wanting to write, may originate in the collective unconscious.

"Until you make the unconscious conscious it will direct your life and you will call it fate." ~ C. G. Jung

The Stories For Stage One

Humpty's Scene One:

To The Wall

His single vanity had always been a gleaming, perfectly elliptical
shell without even the most minute bump, mark, or scratch.

Court's Scene One:

Dad

Making the announcement a second time, at home
to my dad would be the real challenge.

Sylvia's Scene One:

First Heartbreak

"Did your grandmother tell you what
happened after you were born?"

Your Cycle Journey Story:

Scene One - Begin

Humpty's Story Begins

Chapter One: To The Wall

The night before the first day of November Humpty Dumpty hadn't been able to take his eyes off a comet with a sparkling fairy-dust-like tail as it shot across the dark sky. His intuition told him the menacing omen warned of disruptive turmoil about to enter his life.

The next morning Humpty awoke early and dressed with fastidious care. He prided himself on his dedication not to spoil his perfect attendance record at the hatchery—since early May rumors circulated he might be the up and comer in line for the general manager's job when his boss retired.

His single vanity had always been a gleaming, perfectly elliptical shell without even the most minute bump, mark, or scratch. He had a virile grace which attracted whistles and hand clapping from Eggville's younger female eggs.

After dawn on the fateful morning, his best black frockcoat with the Eggville Hatchery crest on the breast pocket wrapped around his shell, he walked out of the families' modernistic gray and red egg carton and looked up at the king's magnificent castle, the only four-story carton in the kingdom. Humpty opened the front of his coat and used his handkerchief to add extra polish to his already gleaming surface. He looked up and spoke to the empty street, "I am the master of my destiny and only need myself to control my fate."

By sheerest chance he glanced down a second time to admire his unrivaled excellence. That singular instant in time Humpty Dumpty felt his yoke curdle and sensed his white turn a shade of gray. He staggered back and uttered a startled cry. "Oh no, oh dear and goodness-gracious, how could this be, there's a crack, a visible fracture in my shell? I'm ruined, brought down and made low and ordinary, so commonplace it staggers my imagination."

He rubbed his eyes and looked again. A minute crack, a detectible flaw, a gruesome mutilation snaked its way down the middle of his shell. His exquisite exterior, the one feature which set him apart, showed an unsightly defect.

Humpty, in the grip of near out-of control panic, grabbed a ladder from the side of the carton and stumbled down the street to the ten-foot high brick wall that for centuries shielded Eggville from the red foxes and other ravenous creatures which roamed the dark forest.

He struggled up the ladder, crawled onto a white-stone ledge and sat down. By now wrinkles and rips dotted his prized frockcoat. He ran his shaking hand over the rough, dark fissure in his prized shell then looked down at the lighting-bolt-shaped fault a second and third time and quivered as paralyzing dread swept over him.

"How can this happen? I'm the cage free egg everyone looks up to, a symbol for shell perfection. A crack just won't do. Until I figure this out nothing is going to get me off the wall."

"Egg, you up there on the wall, they call me Reynard."

Humpty swung around to the forest side of the wall. A fox, its fiery coat shinning and its flame-like tail and ears quivering has amber eyes locked on him.

"Dear, egg, there's no need to fret. I'm a friend, a valuable ally here to help." The predator's soft whine is filled with deadly cunning.

"What's this I see? Horror of horrors, could you possibly have a repulsive crack slicing down the middle of your shell?" The fox's cat-like whiskers vibrate in the breeze as the sly creature puts its front paws on the wall and stands on its hind legs.

"Perhaps I can help. Come down so I can get a better look. There's no time to waste, jump and I'll catch you." A red tongue flicks in and out of the thin mouth and licks the narrow lips.

"In the forest a slight imperfection would go unnoticed. Jump and let me welcome you to a much more forgiving world." The fox's sharp whine crackled with sly energy.

Maybe the panicked Humpty in his state of extreme anxiety doesn't realize the ledge is too narrow. Possibly he's so preoccupied with escaping the fox he pulls back too far and is unnerved by the excited barks, yaps, and high-pitched screams coming from the crafty trickster.

"Why is it I feel woozy?" Humpty tips back and forth and feels his balance desert him. In a desperate attempt to avoid a catastrophic tumble, he grabs the ledge with both hands. Surge after surge of spinning dizziness hits.

He uses every bit of his willpower to tip back. If he falls on the dark forest side of the wall, the fox will make a meal of him. With all his might and a kick of his feet, he screams, struggles and teeters back and forth to regain his balance. Everything goes out of focus. He's over-compensated and it's too late to stop a petrifying plunge.

"No, no, no," Humpty calls out. He topples off the wall, plunging to the ground and hitting with the destructive impact sure to do damage. The too-perfect egg has a fleeting vision of a Dark Night, an ominous black mist with him firmly in its clutches.

He's fallen, been brought down from his perch on the wall, a place that's above it all.

A bolt of pain shoots through his yoke. "Oh my heavens, this is a calamity beyond my imagination. I've taken a terrible tumble. What's going to become of me? First a crack and now these ghastly injuries to my shell, how can I ever live a sunny-side-up life? Torment and woe has overcome me." He feels as shook up as a newly-made omelet.

Tiny, jagged pieces of his shell litter the ground. He shakes his fist at the heavens and cries out, "Curses, fate has betrayed me and misfortune, possibly a magical hex of the worst kind, is upon me. My beautiful, unblemished shell, the elliptical core of my being, my one claim to fame has turned into an unsightly mess. The refinement, charm, and beauty that have been my lifelong companions have deserted me. I am at a point of no return. I'll never be able to put myself together again."

The bell in the steeple of Eggville's clock tower peals nine times. Within minutes eggs on their way to work and school emerge from their cartons. Humpty hears stunned gasps and watches as fingers point at him and the pieces of shell scattered across the ground.

Soon a crowd, including coworkers from the hatchery, rumored to be goose eggs in disguise, a few casual neighborhood acquaintances, the Scramblebergs and the Frymans, and a couple of oversized, know-it-all Ostrich eggs, show up and silently stand over him.

His boss, The Big Egg, pushes through the crowd and looks at the scattered pieces of shell. He runs his stubby finger over the cracks then huffs as he flashes a crooked smile. "Humpty, my boy a cure for your malady is a matter of willpower. Pick up the pieces, patch the cracks the best you can, learn to live with your thoroughly disgusting shell and at least get back to work. Of course, now you're a charity case and I'll have to cut your salary in half." The Big Egg flashes a leering, impatient smile and heads toward the hatchery.

Humpty's wife, Mrs. Dumpty, runs toward her husband. Close to hysterics, she gets down on her hands and knees, wails and tells him, "Dear husband your shell perfection has made you careless. I tell you this great fall is a punishment sent down by the ancient egg gods."

Their neighbor Mrs. Over-Easy tells Humpty he should glue his pieces back in place and make the best of a ruinous situation by joining a circus freak show. A group of passing tea eggs proposes a dubious foreign cure where Humpty hardens his shell by boiling himself in exotic Chinese teas.

Three of the king's ministers, jeweled Faberge eggs on golden, high-kicking steeds, stop and dismount. The egg the others call the Prime Minister, gleaming red rubies dotting his shell, picks up pieces and examines them. He proclaims, "My boy, even the king's men in combination with their horses can't put you together again. King Crumpets needs to know about this. A monstrosity like you could start riots and create a kingdom-wide uprising." The ministers jump on their steeds and with arms waving gallop off in the direction of the castle.

Humpty berates the crowd. "No one, including all the king's horses or all the king's men, has helped. I've had a great fall. Leave, get away from me, I need to be alone."

Humpty states the earliest version of the Humpty Dumpty Principle. "After my terrible tumble, I'm ensnared in the grip of consuming misfortune and if I am to bring grace and purpose back to my life, I must collect the broken pieces and do something about the cracks. I have to find my own way out of this quandary."

Our shocked egg is alone and sitting on the ground. He struggles to comprehend the calamity which has befallen him. Tears stream down his shell.

He has a sudden insight that his Dark Night may have had its origin on a long ago school day when Humpty had drifted off in the middle of a lecture on the egg kingdom's founder, Crumpets the First. His history teacher, Mr. Poach, so old that green moss grew out of his eyebrows, had made an example of him in front of the entire class.

"Dumpty, wake up, you're getting more scrambled every day. That gleaming shell of yours won't ensure success. Pay attention or you'll turn into a bad egg and join one of those deviled egg gangs. That will ruin any possibility of being eligible for the king's highest honor, the *Bon Oeuf* Medal as one of the kingdom's good eggs."

Back in Poach's class he recalls thinking about becoming a deviled egg gang member and deciding if I'm going to turn out to be an undesirable, why even try? Perhaps that day the tide turned against him. Could it be he'd given up and lived his life as a beaten egg? With the fall and the resulting damage, he'd finally met his teacher's dark prediction and his own expectations.

An icy wind blew over his shell. Another childhood confrontation he'd kept in the dark depths of his yoke made its way to the surface. Many years ago, at a Thanksgiving feast, with his twelve egglet brothers and sisters sitting around the table, his father after too many cups of pumpkin-spiced cider, pointed at Humpty and chanted, "My boy is all shell, I have the ideal nickname for him. He'll be our goose egg."

A bitter taste filled Humpty's mouth. He looked back and realized he'd never expected much from himself. The terrible tumble wasn't a shock. In his heart of hearts he knew those dark beginnings were a sign he'd end up being a colossal failure, a fiasco of epic proportions. It had only been a matter of time until he took some kind of a damaging plunge. Why not face facts? The great fall was his lot in life, a fate which couldn't be avoided.

Court's Scene One

Dad

Here's my story without frills or polish.

Moline, where I grew up, is one of a series of Northern Illinois factory towns that line the banks of the Mississippi River. It's a medium-sized hard working, but unimaginative city with more than its share of dingy taverns and neon-signed bowling alleys, which overflow at four in the afternoon, midnight, and eight in the morning when the shifts change at the plants. Every kid grew up knowing they had three choices, work in the mind-numbing factories, take a world-class boring job that supported the factories or get the hell out as fast as possible.

Mom taught school, first grade, at U. S. Grant elementary school, a depression-era, fort-like foreboding structure. The summer away from dad getting her masters degree at the University of Illinois is the only time I ever saw her happy.

Dad's single claim to fame resided in spending a few years in Hollywood working for Art Linkletter, a television host who specialized in interviewing kids. Whenever he felt we doubted his worth, dad pulled out a black and white photo of old Art. He'd tap the picture then hold it up. At the perfect dramatic moment he'd point to himself in a white shirt and tie sitting next to a bigtime entertainer. In a reverential voice he'd tell my brother, mother, and me, "This is Hollywood, a place I once called home."

My earliest memory of dad is resisting and rebelling. It's hard for me to recall anything we agreed upon. To write scene one I traveled back through the years and came to terms with the role he'd played in my life.

The band incident began on a polar cold late October day. On that fateful morning the wind swirled across the frozen football field as banging drums and blaring trumpets produced music vaguely resembling John Philip Sousa's Washington Post March. The unharmonious notes mixed with shouts of "left, right, left right, you're out of step. Band practice sucked worse than a math quiz. My rebellion would begin a few minutes after ten when I'd quit. It would be executed with the precision of a general planning a battle that could win the war.

Louie De Luis, the five foot marching band director at Calvin Coolidge junior high school had a military attitude like an out-of-control Napoleon commanding troops. Again and again, in a vain effort to achieve marching perfection we paraded back and forth across the fifty yard line. The feel of his jackhammer-like hand pounding on my shoulder is still with me. "One, two, three, four, son get with the program. You're still out of step and off the beat."

After practice, precisely the way I'd imagined it, I set an oversized baritone sax case, which could have passed for a gangster's dead body container, in front of De Luis and kicked it over so it hit the floor with a thud. The little creep, his lower lip twitching, stared at me and shook his head.

I delivered my speech the way I'd rehearsed it. "Okay Mr. De Luis, I have no sense of rhythm and I'm out of step and proud of it." He stumbled back sort of the way you would if you thought someone had a psychotic break. I gave him my gunslinger glare. "I quit." And said it loud enough for everyone in the band room to hear.

He took another step back, glared at me and growled out his reply. "Johnson, you're a no-talent loudmouth punk. You quitting my band, that's not the way it works. I'm the one tossing you out."

I locked eyeballs with De Luis, gave him my best smirk, and my snappy about face brought stunned gasps from the band members around us. Without looking back, I marched, probably for the first time in step and on the beat, out of the practice room.

Quitting wouldn't be the hard part of the day. Making the announcement a second time, at home to dad would be the real test of courage. There's a classic TV show with a wise, caring father, *Father Knows Best*. Dad must have been his evil twin and the two words which least described him were wise and caring.

Ever since sixth grade he had this peculiar obsession about me playing in the school band—something about believing he could pass on his natural musical ability. The problem, which didn't make any difference to dad, is I have no sense of rhythm, total zero.

A bad temper didn't come close to rating as Dad's worst problem. He had his own major league childhood trauma. The story I heard from my mother is after a two-day bender his abusive stevedore father used his belt to give him a world-class beating. Then my inebriated granddad, with my sobbing father following, staggered down to the Mississippi River where he managed to climb to the top of a railroad bridge. At the highest point on the span gramps shouted, "The hell with you all," and committed suicide by high diving into the freezing river. A year ago I'd asked dad what happened. Without a word he'd turned and walked out of the room.

Dad's world view never included being faithful. For as long as I could remember he had a lady friend, Madge, the cosmetics clerk at a local drugstore. Once every six weeks or so he took business trips. My mother, brother, and I knew and approved—we'd second any activity to get him out of the house. Our ignoring his philandering didn't mean we could keep a straight face when he left. He'd never had a regular job and business trips seemed the ultimate overreach.

We lived in a small white-framed bungalow and ate dinner in a kitchen my mother, brother, me, and dad barely squeezed into. Dad sat at the head of our kitchen table and chain-smoked Camel after Camel. In between hacking coughs he fumed about blacks, Jews, communists, uppity liberals, and unnamed, dark forces conspiring against the right thinkers. His defense against what he saw as a world where the cards had been stacked against him centered on his nightly ritual of pointing out the faults of my mother, brother, and me, his oldest son.

We'd nicknamed his table time fuming the night court. He'd perch in his chair at the end of the table, waves of nose-numbing Old Spice Cologne pouring off him. He'd hold his cigarette out so he could shove his Spam slices into his mouth. Some nights his garbled rant would go on until bedtime. He'd usually bring his nightly harangues to an end by pointing out and mocking our faults.

That night I sat down at the table, waited until he started to light up and blurted out the sentence that changed mine and dad's life. "I quit the band." My words rang through the deathly silent kitchen.

The Camel bobbed up and down before it dropped into the bowl of steaming stewed tomatoes. Dad gagged and struggled to get his breath.

His eyes went weirdly wide. He ran his hand through his Vitalis soaked hair—he believed the tonic would keep him from going bald—and gawked at me. Before he could recover, I followed up, "I hate playing an overgrown sax. I'm no good and I'm never going back."

Mom, sensing the coming battle, broke into tears. My bawling brother ran into the bedroom. Dad swiped his shaking hand across the table and knocked his favorite plate, the one with an American flag on the top, across the kitchen. It hit the far wall with a crack and shattered. Pieces banged against the gas stove.

He sprang out of his chair. His eyes stuck out of his jackal-like face. He took his time lighting a new Camel, inhaled a deep drag, leaned over and, his nose inches from mine, pounded his fist on the table. Before that night I'd never heard his voice quiver. "First thing tomorrow morning you're going to find Mr. De Luis, get down on your knees, apologize and beg him to take you back."

"No!" I stood up. My chair tipped over and bounced off the side wall. For the first time I could remember I wasn't afraid of him. Everything I'd held back came out. "You're a crummy Neanderthal bigot" Neanderthal had been the week's vocabulary word. "What's more the only thing I hate worse than the stupid sax is smoking."

He sneered and brushed ashes off his undershirt. "Damn quitter. It's just like football, you play in the line because you don't have the talent to be quarterback."

I didn't respect much about dad, but I never lost sight of the fact he had extraordinary critical abilities. The man could find fault at a nun's convention. In two or three sentences he'd tear down the most carefully built self-esteem.

We were inches from each other. I'd never attacked him before that night. This time I let loose the resentment which built up for years. My recollection is still crystal clear how the bitter words spewed out like toxic waste. "You're the one who's a world-class loser."

Coughing and spitting like he was having a fit, he raised his hand to slap me. My mother stood up. "William, sit down!"

Dad reeled back, pounded his fist against the wall and stormed out of the kitchen.

At the next dinner the moment dad sat down my brother threw up on his fried liver. The next four or five months Dad and I got by with grunts and nods. We spent every meal trying to stare each other down. It wasn't hard to figure he expected me to back off.

I didn't and that long ago night I grew up a couple of years in a few seconds. The night courts stopped. Dad retreated to his bedroom and I arranged it so I got home in time for a warmed up dinner and bed. Dad and I rarely spoke and when we did it was out of necessity. Most of our communication got filtered through my mother.

Dad never changed. If anything, he turned darker. Sometimes, when he wasn't on his increasingly long business trips, I'd hear him late at night in his bedroom, his raspy, guttural voice making him sound like a psycho, as he swore and cursed to the heavens about his rotten life and disappointing son.

Nine years after I quit the band dad died from lung cancer. I wouldn't go see him in the hospital and looking back I know I should have made the effort. The way I figured it is that's the one time I showed less class than him.

Until he passed away I kept my own counsel. My outburst gave dad a wake-up call—hearing the truth forced him to look in the mirror and see himself, warts and all. I don't think he could handle the shock.

Today, usually late at night, I imagine hearing dad's smoker's cough followed by a cruel laugh. His ghostly voice taunts me, "Boy, can't you see the day you quit the band ruined your life? What's more every one of your problems is a punishment for not listening to me."

To end this scene I wrote about how I felt about dad.

DAD

My Mad Dad, I wouldn't get up close if I were you,
I'm the one who knows the damage he can do.
My Bad Dad is a looming shadow lying in wait,
Take him on and you're tempting fate.
My Sad Dad is filled with desolation and despair,
Hear my warning, watch out and beware,
Of my Mad Dad, Bad Dad, Sad Dad.

To move past this scene I spent most of a day doing my best trying to imagine what it must have been like to be him. That's the first time I realized how much suffering he'd gone through to end up with such a bleak and angry view of life. Today I accept deep inside he loved me, it's just that he had no idea how to express any feelings outside of rage. Boyhood abuse imprisoned dad in his own Dark Night.

That long ago dinner I could only see the fear dad showed to the world. It took decades of adult experience to realize there's a flipside to his kind of uncontrollable fear. What he so desperately wanted to cover up is the part of him that witnessed his father standing on a railroad bridge and cursing the world.

STITCHING – Connecting Scenes One and Two

The lesson I took away from dad and the band is that if I didn't stand up for myself, no one would. Along the way I grew up. High school, college, a Big Ten school, marriage, a couple of kids and a job with a New York publishing company. I wanted something which would feed my creativity and give me a more positive outlook, but it would involve a painful change of direction.

By the time the upheaval shook my life to its foundation, I'd turned into a confirmed outsider, rebel and loner who didn't share feelings and emotions. I kept my own counsel and if I was unhappy or dissatisfied, no one knew about it.

Sylvia's Scene One

First Heartbreak

I Grew Up On The River Ranch
Seeing Myself As A Wild Child
Heartbreak and loss were my best learning opportunities.

It seems like yesterday, the long ago morning at age ten when I learned I'd move away from my grandparents. It's remained my greatest loss and the darkest of dark days. It's also the moment in time where I formed beliefs which influenced so much of the rest of my life.

I walked out on the covered porch that ran across the front of our farmhouse. Strong smells from the dairy barn mixed with the sweet aroma of the flower beds. I stretched my arms and felt a soft breeze caress my face as I looked out on the fields. When I got to heaven it wouldn't be better than this.

Poppie, my grandfather, holding his brown Stetson and in his khaki work clothes, spit a gob of thick brown chewing tobacco into the grass, turned away and reached around to put his rough, red hand on my shoulder. My eyes stayed glued on his fancy silver belt buckle.

Ever since I could remember I'd taken special pleasure in imagining Poppie as one of the cowboy heroes, like Roy Rogers and Gene Autry I spent a quarter to see on black and white movie screens every Saturday. Sometimes, in my best dramatic moments, I'd see myself as the Swiss girl Heidi in the story where she lives in the mountains with her grandfather. My grandfather's gruff exterior matched Heidi's grandfather to perfection.

The sound of love and pain in his deep voice is an emotion I carry to this day. "Your grandmother told you what happened after you were born." I'd nodded. His eyes stayed on the fields. "There's more, something I wanted to tell you myself. Your mother and her new husband will be here in a month. I'm turning the dairy barn into a house for them. You'll live there."

"You'll live there. You'll live there." How could they do this? My grandfather and grandmother never asked what I thought, what's more they didn't seem to care.

My mouth hung open and my heart pounded so hard I expected it to burst through my chest. "Live with my mother and her new husband, my mother left me and I don't know her. You're my parents." My voice quivered. Tears welled up in the corners of my eyes. "It's like you're sending me to a foster home, no, no, I won't go."

It wasn't the miles or minutes or how far away I'd move, I had a choking sense I'd lost my home and freedom. Before that morning I'd never dreamt of talking back to Poppie. He'd been a soldier in World War One and I couldn't imagine anyone being tougher. This time I didn't care, my grandfather had to listen.

He shook his head and didn't look back as he went down the steps and headed toward the barn. Those shattering words, "you'll live there" changed my life.

It had started after dawn when the smell of sizzling bacon drew me to the kitchen. My grandmother, Gaggie, put the bacon on a plate, and sat down at the table. The corners of her mouth turned down. She talked in the quiet voice she used for church. "Sylvia, I want to share a secret about how you came into the world. Years ago your mother fell under the spell of summer love with a handsome sailor. They married before he shipped out. I saw you for the first time in a military hospital, such an unsettling, noisy, and sterile place. You were a beautiful baby, so warm and cozy wrapped in your soft pink blanket, cooing and lying in your mother's arms."

She wiped away tears. I froze. Her fingers drummed on the plate piled high with toast. "In a few hours your brand-new life would change. Your mother couldn't take care of you on her own and Poppie and I didn't have a place for you. Something had to be done. A nice major and his wife agreed to adopt you and promised to love you."

She looked down at the tabletop and took a deep breath. "This was World War II, a time of great uncertainty when life could end quickly. People made instant decisions. At the very last minute your grandfather and I decided you were too precious to let go. We'd raise you as our own, at least until your mother had time to grow up. A year later, after you'd become such a big part of our lives, Poppie went to the courthouse and had your mother's underage marriage annulled."

So what, I got off to a rough start, lots of kids do. My grandmother's story didn't change the undeniable fact she and Poppie were my parents. We'd lived in Central California on the River Ranch, a two-hundred acre cattle ranch in an old farm house Poppie re-built. I played with my dog Shep and pet calf May, took care of the foxes Poppie and I rescued, rode our horse Old Jim, roamed among the big oak trees, and had a fabulous fort where I'd dream up adventures, some days getting lost for hours in nature and my make-believe world.

How could anyone be more my real mother than Gaggie? She'd taught school and she knew almost everything. Each evening I cuddled next to her on the couch and in this magical way she'd make stories from my Jack and Jill magazine come alive.

Neighbors across the peach orchard had a swimming pool where during the summers kids from nearby ranches came to swim. Nothing felt as alive as being hot from running and playing and jumping into the cold water. I'd stay there until my hands were wrinkled and skin blue then with a sigh everyone could hear, throw myself on to the hot cement that circled the pool. By the end of the summer I'd turned tow-headed and brown-skinned.

I'd help Gaggie pick apples, churn butter, and hang the clothes on the line or I'd tag after Poppie while he did his chores. He taught me how to milk cows, taking time to squirt milk into the mouths of the purring cats that expected their daily treat. Didn't Gaggie and Poppie realize they couldn't get along without me? I'd come up with a superlative name for my time on the ranch, the heaven years.

For the rest of the day, I felt so shook up I finally ran outside and stayed in my fort until dark. The finality of my situation hit the next morning when I walked outside and saw Poppie with his toolbox. Later I heard pounding and sawing and knew he'd started to fix up the dairy barn. My fate was sealed.

That night I pulled the covers over my head. The lilacs outside my window with their sweet rose mixed with a hint of vanilla smell calmed me. What could I have done wrong? There wasn't one thing Poppie asked me to do which wasn't accomplished with absolute perfection. I never talked back and I helped Gaggie fix dinner, did dishes, made my bed and got good grades. There had to be a way to change their minds.

The next morning I got up the courage to do whatever I could to make them understand how heartbroken I felt. When I marched into the kitchen and saw their solemn, sad faces every bit of my resolve vanished. I managed a few garbled words before I couldn't speak. Gaggie hugged me and Poppies went out to do chores. The remaining days went by in a blur. No one dared mention me moving.

A couple of months later my mother, her new husband, and I moved into Poppie's small dairy barn—he'd plastered the blocks and converted the inside into a two bedroom house with asphalt tile floors. It's only heat came from a fireplace and an electric heater. The winter cold and summer heat kept me miserable. Not a day went by without me longing to be back with Gaggie and Poppie, my dog Shep, the farm animals, and sitting in my fort making up a new adventure.

Why couldn't they open their eyes and see I'd lost my home and my freedom? After the move I felt alone, like I lived with strangers. No one would ever persuade me that Poppie and Gaggie weren't my real parents. Mysterious, unknowable forces had turned my world upside down. Like a true heroine, I kept my grief locked deep inside and vowed I would never, ever let anyone see the heart wound I'd suffered. To express my grief, I wrote about Poppie:

Ode to the Man

He was my friend,
Always distant and aloof
With dog at his heels and
Hat shading his well-worn face.
He was my friend, He is my strength
To carry on his will
Does overshadow any doubts
That the cards life deals
Can be dealt with now!
Why must he end?
He was my friend, He is my roots.

A few months later a deep cough wouldn't go away. The doctor told my new parents I had asthma and needed to eat different foods. I overheard them talking about the strain of spending extra money for my special foods and I felt even more like I didn't belong.

That first time I learned what it felt like to be powerless is my strongest childhood memory. It taught me not share my innermost feelings and became the way I dealt with emotional trauma. More than that, it's the view which laid the foundation for future Dark Nights.

I grew up and got to know my mother and stepfather. The feeling Gaggie and Poppie were my parents never completely left. My mother and I were closer in age and we ended up having a special relationship. She was like my big sister. I looked like her and became like her, almost as if I was living another version of her life.

Maybe I'd gotten extra lucky. My parents and grandparents loved me. What's more my parents treated me with the same care and love as my younger brother and sister.

Gaggie, Poppie and my parents have passed on. I look back and see Poppie wearing his Stetson and sitting on his horse and tiny, gentle Gaggie on the couch reading her bible. Over time the shock of the move has been replaced by an understanding of how fortunate I am to have had such special and loving parents and grandparents. I know they all meant well and were doing their best to give me a good life.

I've never come to terms with the freedom I lost when I moved from my grandparent's ranch and had to cope with my mother's very different expectations. Instead of being the tomboy my grandfather and grandmother embraced, my mother wanted me to become a young lady, wear the stylish dresses she made for me and play with paper dolls. It seemed like someone waved a magic wand and I'd lost my real self, my alone time and independence. There were new responsibilities, helping take care of the house and later my brother and sister. My mother and new stepfather imposed rules and had social expectations for me, like 4-H sewing club, and piano lessons.

On the River Ranch I'd grown up living in nature on land filled with Oak Trees and wildlife. The contrast of moving into another world with my mother and new family seemed alien.

Recently I read, *The Long Shore* by Jane Hollister Wheelwright, that gave deeper insight into the childhood loss I felt when I left the River Ranch.

Jane grew up in the wilderness on the historic Hollister Ranch that followed the ocean coastline in Santa Barbara County. She writes how when she was older she came to understand the power of being raised in nature and how that realization created a lifelong journey to heal her loss after the ranch was sold. For the first time I found a kindred spirit, someone who understood my deep feeling of loss.

STITCHING –Connecting Scenes One and Two:

I took two emotions away from leaving the River Ranch, a profound sense of losing my home and freedom, and a deep anger that people hadn't considered my feelings. They'd taken away my voice. I grew up living with my parents, followed in my mother's footsteps and went to beauty school, got married and had two daughters. That long ago heartbreak never left. For years I stayed quiet as I struggled to understand why the move impacted me at such a consuming level.

Tell * Journal * Write Your Scene One

A Cycle Journey Story brings resolution to a great fall. How do we know? We've spent the last year using our journeys as models for our stories. The results surprised us. Memories we'd missed or repressed entered our consciousness. We grew into skilled storytellers who could make forgotten times come alive. What's more, we found replaying traumatic scenes in our minds stopped. They'd lost their power over us.

Your Cycle Journey Story isn't about making you the next Faulkner or Hemingway. **What you tell, journal, or write is about insights and awareness not grammar or sentence structure.**

Think of us as coaches giving advice that helps you get the most meaning out of each scene in your story. Throughout the **Tell* Journal * Write** segments we'll suggest ways to put together scenes that combine a Cycle Journey description and the feelings and emotions which inhabit the stages.

At each stage in the journey your goal is to end up with a three to five page scene based on an incident from your life. Stitch the scenes together with connecting paragraphs and the entire Cycle Journey Story would be between thirty and fifty pages.

Scene one, the beginning, is about looking back to your youth. Your objective is to discover the history of the upheaval's formation. You'll tell how the past affects the present by recalling events that created lifelong impressions. Narrow your view. Pick a specific incident. Don't try to describe your whole childhood. Whether you tell it, journal it or write it, a tight scene has the most impact. Allow time for revisions. Most likely your story will come out of the unconscious in bits and pieces.

Add details and specifics, the times, places, and images which relate to your characters. Court's dad had a jackal-like face. Sylvia had her own fort where she could let her imagination run wild.

When you tell, journal, or write your travels through the beginning stage and the other seven stages, you'll release bottled-up feelings and emotions.

Telling your story out loud is a good way to get a feel for an incident from your early life. Pick a friend, wife or husband or significant other, someone you trust, and tell them about an incident from your childhood. If there is no one you feel comfortable sharing with, talk to yourself out loud. To give it needed reality, it's important your story be told in storyteller fashion.

Each time you tell any portion of your story, or are even thinking about how you'll tell the story, have a **Cycle Journey Story Journal**, a notebook where you can write free-form, next to you. You can record repressed memories, which develop the depth that makes a scene meaningful, in the journal. Take days, a week or as long as necessary to build your full scene.

The journal organizes your thoughts and adds detail and realism to scenes. Your unconscious, thoughts you're not consciously aware of, has the time to release its contents in bits and pieces and sudden bursts. The messages sent from the unconscious to the conscious are often mysterious. Be ready to record feelings, insights and other indistinct messages as soon as they come into your mind. They are creative ideas which stimulate your imagination and are often packaged in the form of symbols, metaphors, similes, and analogies.

In your journal draw or write about experiences, dreams, feelings, thoughts, tears, and joys. Use colored pens for a journal drawing. Clip photos or other images to a journal page. Jot down when you feel tense or stumble on sources of conflict. Record inspirations for settings, changes in tone or expanding word choices.

Read diaries or interview family members for backstory options and add their feedback to the journal. Document your personal view—are you angry or have you resolved an old dispute? Dialogue for a scene can come into your mind, include it in the journal.

Your Cycle Journey Story Journal is a creative approach to chronicling thoughts which influence your story. Your unconscious loves attention. **The more you journal, the more you'll receive messages from your unconscious and its shadow.**

Let the words, pictures or symbols flow as new awareness and insights emerge. Whatever you write or draw is okay. You don't have to immediately understand its meaning.

Your beginning scene and other scenes need to contain a combination of objective and subjective views.

The **objective view** is factual. It describes who entered your journey. It could be your parents, a teacher, a relative or a school bully. You're telling who did what to whom, where, when and how how it happened. You pile on details, give locations and tell things that took place. The danger in the objective view is that you tend to tell the same story over and over without coming to any resolution. Be careful, the objective view used repetitively and by itself can turn into nothing more than a long list of complaints that cause you to feel like a victim.

The **subjective view** centers on your perception, your awareness and emotional view you have of people and events. It's built around personal insights about meaningful truths and compelling themes. There's an emphasis on figurative language that reaches into the unconscious to reveal deep changes in feelings and emotions.

Your Cycle Journey Story Journal can be your most effective way to begin to blend together the objective and subjective views.

Your first task in shaping your scene is to use your subjective and objective views to write a **core sentence** that gives shape and direction to the rest of the scene. The concept of a **core sentence** comes from Isaak Dineson, the pseudonym for Karen Cristence Dinesen, Danish novelist and the main character in the movie *Out of Africa*. She had a reputation as an extra-ordinary storyteller. Her guests would supply her with an opening or core sentence and, with their sentence as her starting point, she'd tell a tale that went on for hours.

The core sentence in Court's scene one is, "My rebellion would begin a few minutes after ten when I'd quit and it would be executed with the precision of a general planning a battle that could win the war."

The **action statement** is, "I'd quit."

The **scene theme** is, "my rebellion."

The rest of the beginning scene fulfills the core sentence promise by telling what happens after Court quits the band. The rebellion theme carries through the scene and reappears in other scenes.

The core sentence in Sylvia's scene is, "The morning I learned I'd have to move away from my grandparents is still my greatest loss and the darkest of dark days."

The **action statement** is, "I'd have to move."

The **scene theme** is, "my greatest loss."

The rest of scene one tells of Sylvia moving away from her grandparents. The theme which carries through her story is loss.

You will build a step-by-step progression of insights from a core sentence or phrase and a concise theme ready to serve as a seed for the conscious and the unconscious to establish communication that enlarges and evolves the heart of the scene.

The core sentence can be the opening for how you tell your story or it can set the scene for what you write.

Word choice is critical to your scenes. Words to help you write a beginning scene are:

Wistful	Recall	Earliest Memory
Reflective	Shaped My Life	Travel Back
Contemplative	Look Through Time	My Youth
Forgotten Yesterday	Longing	Melancholy
Recollection	Moment in Time	Past Life

To tap into the full value of the subjective view, **tell how writing the scene affected you by adding a deeper insights and expanded awareness paragraph to your journal.** When you feel it's complete, make it the last paragraph in your scene. Court's final paragraph showed the awareness to see the world from his father's view and develop empathy for his childhood treatment. Sylvia's final paragraph got her in touch with how the move away from her grandparents and losing her freedom affected her.

TWO

The Black Stage, Upheaval

Peace and Harmony Are Destroyed

"There are things that we don't want to happen, but we have
to accept things that we don't want to know but have to learn,
and people we can't live without that we have to let go."

~Author Unknown

An Introduction To Stage Two

The great fall, a terrible tumble, or perilous plunge are different ways to describe an upheaval. This is a turmoil-filled change catalyst that demands a response. It collapses parts or all of the structure of your life. An upheaval is also the start of your journey toward a transformational experience.

In The Essentials we'll define upheaval and give examples of the damage it can do. There are movies like *Ordinary People* and *The King's Speech* that reveal how upheaval exists in our culture. Then comes a Deeper Insight into the shadow, the part of your unconscious where you hold repressed thoughts, along with the ultimate possibilities for your future. Next there are the stories. Humpty is still recovering from his fall, Court has been shocked by his divorce, and Sylvia is reeling from a sliding house.

Stage Two ends with Tell * Journal * Write coaching where you get advice on how to describe the chaos and turmoil of upheaval.

The Essentials

Think of an upheaval as an earthquake which brings a tremor-filled shaking of your life. For an egg or a person the black stage's upheaval or head-over-heels fall is an intense, unnerving shock with the power to break apart life and leave behind confusion, conflict, anxiety, commotion, and hostility, the ingredients that create a Dark Night.

For another person the same onslaught barely registers as a tremble and becomes an absorbing test. No time is wasted confronting the upheaval's challenges. These people put their energy into coming up with life-changing solutions.

Differences in reactions to any personal quake originate in varied life experiences. For the event to be upgraded to an upheaval with the power to set off a Dark Night, the loss and disorientation need to be viewed as significant.

Symptoms of upheaval that brings a Dark Night are:

- The quake takes away ordinary existence. Your world is so shaken there seems to be no way to get back to your old life.
- Upheaval chaos is disorienting and fear producing.
- Significant tension and conflict erupt out of the quake. Over-stressed relationships often break apart. There's a search for someone else to blame.
- Upheaval tension creates temper flare ups over small inconveniences.
- Sleeplessness, forgetfulness, and confusion are common.
- The disturbance and disorder create a panic which brings a yearning for change.
- There's a buildup of sorrow, grief and regret.

Individuals, families, and communities can be changed in profound ways by upheaval. Nine-eleven introduced violent social and political change along with deep Dark Night distress and became a turning point in fighting terrorists. Hurricane Katrina, a sudden wide-spread disaster for New Orleans affected the entire city and, along with help from across the nation, the city rebounded by constructing thousands of new homes. The Newtown shootings were an unimaginable tragedy and a grievous Dark Night wound which brought family and national misery and led the mourning parents to become passionate advocates for reforming gun laws.

At first everything about the upheaval sounds dismal and grim. Another possibility arises when life is shaken up. **The upheaval and accompanying Dark Night serve as an attention-getting shock necessary to let us know we have to change our old way of approaching life.**

The novel and movie *Ordinary People* is the story of a Lake Forest, Illinois family, a son, mother and father, facing a tragic upheaval, the darkest Dark Night. The eldest son, Buck, drowned while he and his brother were sailing on Lake Michigan. Conrad, his depressed brother attempts suicide and after months in a psychiatric hospital, is being treated by a psychiatrist. Calvin and Beth, the parents, are trapped in dark depression and doubt their long-held traditional views of the world. The compelling story tells how this upheaval spins outward and changes many lives forever. It also illustrates how families or groups, even though changed forever, find new ways to deal with their lives, while others cannot escape the upheaval's turmoil.

A very different view of an upheaval Dark Night is presented in Herman Melville's great American novel *Moby Dick*. In this tale of obsession, Captain Ahab represents an ultimate fanatical, madness-fueled reaction to an upheaval. He's morbid, driven, and consumed by his Dark Night. He states his rage when he says, "From hell's heart I stab at thee, for hate's sake I spit my last breath at thee. Ye dammed whale."

No matter what the cost, he will force his crew to become part of his insane plan to get his revenge on the white whale for biting off his leg. To put his white whale obsession in perspective and show how an upheaval is an individualized experience, in Ahab's time whalers understood their profession carried great risk. For many sailors the loss of a limb served as a symbol of the cost of being a whaler and after they lost an arm or leg, the sailor moved on with stoic New England determination. Not Ahab, he's in a full-blown, insanity-driven Dark Night turmoil. He's turned monomaniacal, possessed with an obsessive zeal to prove, despite the danger to his crew, it's his fate to put a harpoon into Moby Dick's blubber. His upheaval-fueled arrogance makes him an ideal candidate for a self-destructive over-reaction.

Personal upheavals or great falls resulting in Dark Nights like Ahab's or in *Ordinary People* are marked by what is perceived as extreme individual loss, injuries or limitations devastating enough to bring the victim's normal life to a halt. They might spring from heartbreak tied to the end of a special relationship, an unexpected loss of a home or a job or fear of aging. Dark Night turmoil can also erupt out of sustained conflict and unresolvable quarrels, or originate in feeling unfilled or purposeless.

The movie *The King's Speech* shows how an upheaval and its Dark Night initiates a Cycle Journey. In 1925 Prince Albert, the Duke of York and second son of King George V and a severe stutterer must give the opening speech at the British Empire Exhibition at Wembly Stadium. He seizes up and can't make the words come out. Albert viewed the failed speech as a crippling disorder. Rather than suffer further embarrassment, he gives up any hope of a cure. He believes he's trapped in a Dark Night and he'll never find a voice of his own. He states the frustration of finding a way to express inner pain when he says, "Because I have a right to be heard! I have a voice!"

He wanders, going through every kind of speech therapist imaginable until he meets the unconventional Lionel Logue and begins a quest to master his stuttering and find his voice. He learns to accept and proclaim he can take over from his brother Edward when he abdicates the throne. In 1939, with Britain entering World War II, he transforms and, with firmness and resolve gives a radio speech to rally his country.

Not every Dark Night is as profound or deadly as Ahab chasing the whale or as overpowering as *Ordinary People* struggling to survive a great tragedy. Other upheavals and Dark Nights, as shown in *The King's Speech*, are a necessary part of claiming an authentic destiny.

Stage 2 Deeper Insight Your Shadow

"The shadow is a moral problem that challenges the whole ego personality, for no one can become conscious of the shadow without considerable moral effort. To become conscious of it involves recognizing the dark aspects of the personality as present and real. This act is the essential condition for any kind of self-knowledge."
~ C. G. Jung

Overcoming the great fall means working with what has been driven out of consciousness and into your shadow. This part of our unconscious is not evil or alien and adds necessary depth to our personality. The shadow holds what has been pushed away or repressed and hides what we consider unacceptable, baser feelings like lust, selfishness, greed, envy, or rage. What we deny in ourselves, deem undesirable or beyond our reach is drawn into its darkness.

Decisions have two obvious choices, there is one way and there is another. The shadow represents the other way, every alternative choice in each of our decisions. Take out a coin and lay it on a table. One side is up and the other side is down and out-of sight. The shadow is the down side, the side you know is there, but can't be seen. Choose hard-boiled and you won't show the flip side, empathy. Be cheerful and don't show the hidden glum and moody part of you.

There is a third, more subtle choice.

You can picture the whole coin, the side in the light and the side in the dark.

Another shadow aspect is the undecidable decision where you love and hate something or someone at the same time—as you often do with a parent or in a close relationship. This contradiction is unresolvable and you push it into the shadow.

Imagine the shadow as a part of your denied expression and kept in a dark closet. In Doctor Jekyll and Mr. Hyde, Edward Hyde represented the shadow of saintly Doctor Henry Jekyll, the dark part of him which escaped into the real world.

The shadow also holds positive life choices, opportunities so challenging fear pushes them into the darkness—your scenes help bring them into consciousness.

The shadow exerts the most power in the first four stages. The beginning holds unsettling childhood memories pushed into the shadow. Upheaval contains shadow fears that must be given a voice in trauma, and in wandering the ability to find a meaningful quest entails drawing self-imposed limitations out of the shadow. In the cycle's later stages, completing the quest and acceptance and proclaiming its results often forces the quester to confront decades-old shadow beliefs.

The Stories For Stage Two

Humpty's Scene Two:

Beyond Repair
"The world has turned dark and dismal."

Court's Scene Two:

Divorce Remorse
The blackest mood I could ever remember had me in its grip.

Sylvia's Scene Two:

Lost Home
An awful crack, a spine-tingling, cardrum-splitting sound which so often starts a disaster movie, echoed through the house.

Your Cycle Journey Story:
Scene Two - Upheaval

Humpty's Story Continues:
Chapter Two: Beyond Repair

Full of fear, Humpty puts his hands over his eyes as he braces himself against the ladder. He can't shake his disbelief over the great fall. "Turmoil rules my life. My dark distress overwhelms me. I am forsaken and nothing but sadness and despair is left. The world has turned dark and dismal. My only chance for redemption is to go over the wall and try to talk some sense into the foxes."

He steps onto the ladder's first rung, puts his hands on the sides as he imagines the deadly predators beyond the wall. Even if he can convince the foxes, there will be the grasping roots of one of the ancient trees or the prickling thorns of a poison bush. Those threats pale in comparison to the rumors of snakes, jackals, and giant-sized rats roaming the darkest parts of the forest.

Humpty shakes his damaged shell. "What choice do I have?" He starts to pull himself up.

One of Dad Dumpty's daily lectures comes into his mind. "My boy, with a stunning outer surface being your only advantage in the kingdom, you must come to grips with how fragile eggs are. You don't think things through and that makes you far too reckless. Someday your luck will run out. Damage your glorious shell and there's nothing left. You're as fried as fried gets."

He remembers how his mother, her fancy lace apron wrapped around her extra, extra large shell, waited patiently for Dad Dumpty to finish his fatherly advice before she kissed her son's shell. "Dear, listen to your father. Eggs who are careless don't have a long life. You must shun even the possibility of risk."

Humpty faces the sobering reality his freakish appearance has taken away any chance to be successful. "What hope is there?" His foot quivers as he climbs another step.

That's the moment he experiences a flash of clarity. It's not in the nature of Reynard and the other foxes to listen to a reasoned appeal. They'll sink their teeth into him before he has a chance to say a word.

No options are left. What use would there be in trying to return to his job at the hatchery? It's a snobby place where advancement depends on appearance. Cracks and missing pieces would ruin any chance at the general manager's job. Just a month ago Quintin, a gull egg in accounting, was quietly let go when a customer complained about too many unsightly bumps in his shell. Humpty takes a third step.

Reynard calls out, "You've finally gotten sensible egg. What harm could possibly befall you if you climbed over the wall and the two of us simply had a chat? I give you my word you'll be as safe as safe can be. After all, we are neighbors. Hurry, please hurry." Humpty hears slobbering as the fox licks its lips.

"Don't listen to a devious fox dear husband. He'll gobble you down before your feet touch the ground. What would the egglets and I do without you? Please, please come down." Humpty looks down. His sobbing wife and his six egglets are at the bottom of the ladder. She's right. His horrid appearance has affected his judgment. He climbs down and embraces his wife. On the other side of the wall Reynard's barks, yelps, and lets loose howls.

Mrs. Dumpty dries her tears and forces a smile. "Dearest husband, I have a wonderful idea, a plan to make you just as good as you were before your fall. The answer to all our troubles is back at the carton. Stay here and promise me you'll not climb back on the ladder."

Humpty nods and Mrs. Dumpty and the egglets run in the direction of their carton. A half-hour later Humpty's wife is waving and coming toward him. She's holding a hand mirror, a red tube, and a bright pink box. The six distraught egglets are a few steps behind.

She grins and proudly holds up the tube. "It's Ajax Super Glue." Humpty shakes his head.

She waves the pink box in front of him. "Actor's pancake makeup." Humpty shrugs his shoulders. His wife isn't making sense.

"Don't you see, we'll glue on the missing pieces and put makeup on the cracks?"

At his wife's insistence Humpty picks up a few jagged shell pieces and does his best to glue them back on his shell. One glance in the hand mirror tells him the glue streaks all over his shell make him look worse than having missing pieces. He dabs makeup on the cracks, takes another look and realizes the folly of his wife's suggestions. "I look ridiculous, like one of the clown eggs at the Easter egg hunts."

He pats Mrs. Dumpty's shell. "No covering is going to camouflage my monstrous exterior. I'm the spitting image of a Frankenstein egg. I've been watching you and the egglets keep your eyes on the ground and I can hear the egglets whispering. They're afraid to tell me they're embarrassed by my awful shell."

"It's a terrible predicament." His wife moans as she and the egglets weep and wail. "Admit it dear husband, especially with the king's ministers seeing you, our lives are ruined—certainly any chances at success are gone."

Mrs. Dumpty turns away. "As much as I love you, we have to face facts. Your tumble changed our lives. We could lose our carton and end up living in one of the abandoned chicken coops. I'm at a loss, it all seems hopeless. For our sake you must try to make the best of it." Humpty's wife takes his hand and leads him back to their carton.

Early the next morning, as the rooster crows a realization comes to Humpty. His yoke has probably gone flat and his white may be on the verge of turning runny. He becomes aware of a new reality. Soon he'll soon be labeled a rotten egg and be seen as the same kind of a freak as the turkey egg born with a square shell. He tells himself, "The king's ministers couldn't help, dad's advice is worthless, I don't believe in fortune tellers, my wife tried her best and failed to give me hope and the egglets think I'm a freak. Probably, after one bite, even Reynard would find me unappetizing. My life has lost its meaning. The great fall is turmoil from which I cannot recover."

Court's Scene Two

Divorce Remorse

I had to leave. In my shocked, shaky state I looked at this upheaval as a radical change that already brought disorder and pain to my life.

Divorce uproar drained me. Upstairs my soon to be ex-wife's heart-wrenching sobs and the whimpers of my kids made leaving so much worse. I opened the door and freezing Chicago air hit like a slap in the face. The goodbye line qualified as the dumbest ever. "See you later."

The blackest mood I could ever remember had me in its grip. I'd promised myself I'd learn from my father's example and I'd failed miserably. I'd been unfaithful and my running around destroyed our marriage. Worse than her disillusionment the thought I'd ended up just like my father left me more depressed and disillusioned.

Outside my freezing breath drifted away from the house. In my numb state I barely felt the cold. I tossed my suitcase into the trunk of the black Chevrolet. For years I traveled, leaving on Monday morning and coming back late on Friday. This time leaving was different. I might never return to my home again.

The engine chugged, sputtered and struggled against the grip of sub-zero temperatures. A way-too-cheerful voice on the car radio announced, "Morning commuters, you're day of reckoning has arrived. It's mid-February and old man winter is huffing and puffing all over Chicago. For those of you foolish enough to venture outside (the pause built suspense) the wind chill just hit twenty below."

The gray, desolate landscape reflected my bleak mood, but I didn't need frigid scenery to feel fearful and depressed. A week of non-stop fighting ended with us agreeing to divorce. My wife wanted me out of the house before noon.

I backed down the driveway and imagined dad's gloating words ringing in my ears. "Well, well Mr. I Quit the Band, it's no surprise you've racked up another failure. Like I always said, my son is a screw up. Face it, you don't have what it takes to stick with it."

For the past decade we'd lived in Clarendon Hills, a Chicago suburb, an idyllic village with good schools and block after block of picture-perfect families. I'd made a half-hearted attempt to fit in, but I'd spent most of my time wishing I lived in the city.

The pulling apart happened gradually, so slowly I don't think either of us could see it coming. We lived in different worlds. I'd worked for a college publisher and my friends were professors at Big Ten schools. She lived in suburbia and had little or no interest in what a professor thought of our latest economics textbook. My trips got longer, her bridge games became more important and the gap between us widened each year.

On this impossibly frigid day my life reached a crossroad. I'd take a last flight. Maybe, after today the jet plane symbol would stop plaguing me.

Dazed and feeling numb I drove from the western suburbs past the imposing McDonalds world headquarters, looking like it wanted to tell me I couldn't measure up to Midwestern family standards, and maneuvered onto the expressway to O'Hare Airport. In bumper-to-bumper traffic filled with commuters beeping horns and gauging their chances of not freezing to death, regret and fear, signs I'd made a final pivot away from stability, took hold. O'Hare appeared in the distance. Overhead I heard the roar of jet engines and imagined travelers escaping to Florida or, like me California. Somehow, in an emotional fog I parked the car and with a frozen face and numb hands and feet, ran for the airport terminal. An hour later, after stumbling through the check-in line and looking less connected than a newly made zombie, I boarded the plane to the coast.

We took off. I looked down at the Sears Tower and wondered how long it would be until I saw Chicago again. My only recollection of the flight is staring out the window and watching clouds drift by. By the time we landed in LA, my anxiety felt like a hundred pound weight on my chest. I had to force myself out of the seat.

Exhausted and lightheaded, I put together enough incoherent mumbling to rent the car for the drive up the coast. For the next five hours my moods shifted at supersonic speed. One moment I'd be angry and pounding on the steering wheel. The next minute I'd look out at the ocean and be so panicked and jumpy I had to pull over and take deep breaths.

In an emotional fog I drove past Malibu, Ventura, and north to Santa Barbara where I found a beach a few miles outside town and walked in the sand until the sun set. I'll never forget the dark water, listening to the churning waves and wondering if I could be anymore at loose ends.

The first night when the cold winds started to blow off the ocean I went back to the car felt exhaustion hit and like a homeless nomad, crawled in the back seat and tried to sleep. My eyes closed I found myself back in Chicago condemned by some nameless righteous entity to spend endless days trapped in the airport listening to faceless, pious looking bystanders shout in my face. "We're giving you an award for making a total mess out of your life. And we're sentencing you to spend eternity in the storm of chaos you created."

The next morning, in a depression-fueled funk, I drove back to Santa Barbara. For reasons I didn't want to try and understand and without the slightest idea what my room cost, checked into the Biltmore, fanciest hotel in town. For four days, as one sunny afternoon blended into the next, I'd get up, stand in the shower and go over and over how my marriage dissolved.

Each time I shaved and looked in the mirror, I'd see myself as broken beyond repair. Even worse my kids wouldn't have anything to do with me. I'd screwed up in a world-class way.

The afternoons went by with me sitting next to an Olympic-sized pool a towel wrapped around my shoulders and doing my best to look like a movie star on vacation. Most of my energy went into thinking of ways to make things right. I'd imagine calling my soon to be ex-wife and begging for forgiveness, and pleading for a second chance. I must have called six or seven times. Each time she answered I hung up.

I'd made a complete wreck of my life and felt like a disaster survivor. For as long as I could remember I'd had no passion for anything but protecting myself. That's as dark a view of life as it's possible to have. Maybe I could find another way and maybe I'd gotten a special delivery message that I could do more than push people away.

Reality hit hard when the hotel stuck a bright yellow copy of my bill under the door. I'd been spending money I didn't have. Still without a clue what to do next, I paid my bill, got in my car, drove back to the airport and on a spur of the moment inspiration brought a ticket to my hometown. I'd stay with my mother for a while.

I'd left my home, been on a plane, slept on a beach and wandered around an expensive hotel. Why did all those different settings seem like the same place, probably because they were? I'd put myself in a netherworld between two lives. My old one had broken beyond repair. A new one where I could claim a brighter future I couldn't yet see.

At my mother's home, the same old white-framed bungalow where dad and I had gone at it, I rarely slept more than a few hours. Every time I'd close my eyes a crushing sense of defeat would sweep over me. One nightmare had me alone in an old city where the broken buildings lined streets littered with dead bodies. The dream left me so shaken I stood in a cold shower for a half hour. For two months my only solace came from going back to places where I'd grown up, even walking up and down the field where I played high school football and wishing I could go back and start over.

One morning I woke up with a stunning insight. I said it out loud, "My marriage is over. I don't have anything to lose, there's nothing to stop me from doing whatever I want. This could be a second chance, the best opportunity I'll ever have to see if I can find a life with a meaning beyond protecting myself."

I wrote down my choices. I could start a company. I had experience as a speaker and I'd done some training. I could teach. I always wanted to write, maybe this was the time. For the first time I felt excited about the future. The next day, full of enthusiasm and with a new awareness of life's possibilities, I said goodbye to my mother, got on a plane and headed back to California, this time with a commitment to find a new direction for my life.

STITCHING – Connecting Scenes Two and Three

Upheaval offers two choices. Become part of the turmoil or make the changes necessary to move forward. I returned to California ready to get my life back on track. It wasn't hard to find a sales job. Dating proved to be a bigger challenge. I'd gotten married right after college and I didn't have much experience. I moved in with the first girl I dated twice. We lived in a nice beach house. Outside appearances didn't match relationship reality. Month by month the tension and conflict escalated. The tremors signaled a second upheaval.

Sylvia's Scene Two

Lost Home

An awful crack, a spine-tingling, eardrum-splitting sound echoed through the house. I had a sense of loss, like a premonition my world would soon be upended. I'm getting ahead of myself.

The catastrophe began a year after a devastating divorce. I slept and cried, which got me fired from a beauty college job. Just as I had done when my grandparents told me I'd have to move, I'd stayed quiet and kept my pain to myself. Then my girls came down with chicken pox. Completely overwhelmed by this onslaught of crippling turmoil, I did the only thing I could and left them with my mother and grandmother while they healed.

I felt like the star of my own soap opera and knew I needed a way to turn off the drama. One winter morning at the local coffee shop my past took a giant leap in the direction of catching up with my present. My friend Jake, who'd given me a job in his beauty salon and who had just finished his divorce, reached across the table and took my hand. "Sylvia, you want to start over. My mother owns a lot in a small mountain community. She's willing to give it to me to build a home and start a new life."

The pain behind my forehead felt like a lightning bolt being born. Should I uproot the children and myself or in my emotionally fragile state try to take care of myself and the girls? I took the biggest gamble of my life and we went with him.

So my daughters would have a place to sit and there would be room for our belongings, he traded in his Jaguar for a four-door Chevy Camaro. On a New Year's Day with the sun shining and the temperature in the mid-seventies we left for the mountains. If we had an inkling of the coming disasters, none of us would have gotten in Jake's car.

We built a house on the edge of the steep hill that had a stunning valley view and stayed comfortable and warm. The day of the slide the worst blizzard in years hit the mountains. Hundreds of tourists and locals were stranded. Between angry black clouds and blinding snow it got so bad planes airlifted in supplies and volunteer firemen with four-wheel drive vehicles delivered provisions.

Mid-morning Jake, who worked as a volunteer fireman, headed for the fire station. The girls were home and in the middle of an ultra-competitive Monopoly game, with accusations of not playing by the rules and game pieces, money, hotels and houses being tossed across the floor. The smell of my biscuits filled the house and a pot of beef stew started to bubble. It felt wonderful to be warm, cozy, and safe.

A shot-like cracking noise echoed through the house. My head snapped around. I looked in the direction of the unearthly sound. A long, jagged, vertical crack ran from the top to the bottom of the stairs.

I staggered back, took deep breaths and rushed to the stairwell. No damage. I ran downstairs. No cracks in the bedrooms.

Maybe we were lucky the house hadn't caved in on our heads. I hurried upstairs. My hands shook as I dialed the fire station and pulled myself together enough to sound calm. "Jake, I heard this awful noise, horrible creaking and groaning. A jagged crack running from the top to the bottom of the stairs, appeared in the wall. It feels like the house is breaking apart."

We'd been talking for a minute when a second creaking, groaning darkly ominous reverberation more ear splitting than the first and loud enough for Jake to hear over the phone, boomed through the house. I screamed and dropped the phone. The icy cold fear you get when you sense your life is in danger brushed over me.

Jake yelled, "Guys, my home, it's ready to slide down the hill. Let's go."

He paused a second then told me, "Sylvia, turn off the gas, get dressed, get the girls in their warmest clothes, pack what you can and get out of there. We'll be there in ten minutes." Before he hung up I heard sirens.

A couple of hours later the girls and I were safe at the fire station. Jake and the volunteers worked until after dark wrapping a huge steel cable around the house and securing it to three nearby pine trees and a couple of telephone poles.

Our house, steel cable and all sat deserted through the long winter. We moved into Jake's aunt and uncle's summer cabin. It had a fireplace, stove and oven, and no other heat. Through a long mountain winter we slept in ski clothes and under sleeping bags. Every day I trudged through the snow to my beauty salon, where I had enough work for us to buy food and supplies.

In April when the snow melted, we had to declare the home a total loss. Our insurance wouldn't cover any of the damage. We lost most of our possessions. Jake gave the house back to the builder. He took over the loan, fixed it and moved in, but never could sell what became known as the sliding house.

As dark as this sounds, my daughters remember that winter as a marvelous adventure. Snow covered the steep roof and drifted to the ground. They'd sled from the top of the cabin down the driveway. While we worried and struggled to survive the long, turmoil-filled winter of the house which refused to stay in one place, their laughter provided the only bright spot in our lives,.

The deeper insight I took away from the sliding house is the feeling I didn't belong in the mountains. I loved the forest and the beautiful sunsets, but it seemed like I'd forgotten to notice fate doesn't like it when you don't pay attention to its warnings.

STITCHING – Connecting Scenes Two and Three:

Security is an illusion. In an instant our lives can crumble around our feet. The mountains and the sliding house taught me I needed to enjoy each day for that unique experience and not take anything for granted. Almost from the first day my intuition told me I didn't belong in the mountains and, if I stayed things would get worse. I refused to give in. It wasn't long until I learned it can be disastrous not to listen to your intuition.

Tell * Journal * Write

Scene Two

As coaches we've discovered how to tell the story of an upheaval stage by spending the better part of a year going over and over our own great falls. It's emotionally taxing, but it's the start of the self-understanding you need to write your Cycle Journey Story.

For scene two imagine a person looking out on a landscape ravaged by earthquake destruction as a metaphor for upheaval's destructive power. Whether you're telling, journaling, or writing, your scene needs to show how your life has been shaken or shattered by this bleak turmoil. Think about the sensations you experienced—anger, crying, maybe an upset stomach or blinding headaches. **If you can connect with upheaval feelings and emotions, scene two will take on a new level of reality.**

As you did in the beginning scene, begin with a strong **core sentence** that tells how an upheaval brought unrest and confusion to your life. Court's core upheaval sentence is, "I had to leave and in my fragile mental state I looked at this upheaval as a radical change that brought disorder and chaos to my life." "I had to leave" is the action driving the scene and "radical change that brought disorder and chaos" is the theme running through much of Court's story.

Your challenge is to describe its confusion, swaying emotions, and agitation by establishing the right tone.

Think of tone as the manner or style you'll choose to express the stages' character and feeling. The tone lets the scene unfold through your eyes. It establishes a personal outlook and evokes the strength of your feelings and emotions.

The tone, which can unexpectedly change or remain constant, can be foolish, nasty, ironic, sad, serious, fearful, depressed, relaxed, or threatening. Every adjective and adverb, even the way you structure sentences, becomes part of the scene's tone.

A good way to get a sense of tone is to see how it plays out in all the stages.

- **Beginning** tone is one of discovery as youthful events are looked at through adult eyes. Let the childlike emotions come through, but interpret them with an adult view.
- **Upheaval** where the great fall happens has a chaotic and turmoil-filled quality.
- **Trauma** is about the struggle to find a voice to express sadness and inner pain.
- **Wandering** tone must feel aimless and lost.
- **Quest** introduces an attitude of purpose and commitment and waiting destiny.
- **Acceptance** is an interaction with the inner critic and advocate presenting concerns and encouragements.
- **Proclaiming's** climate is filled with the fear a new destiny won't be accepted.
- **Transformation**, discovering a new you, is built on surprise and delight.

Read Court's scene one and feel his growing rebellion. Phrases like "demented monarch," "pointing out our faults", "night court," and "find fault at a nun's convention," set the tone of a child protecting the Self with a full-blown revolt.

Your word choice is the best way to reflect an upheaval feeling. Try words and phrases like:

Fragile Mental State	Major Mayhem	Feeling Numb
Uproar	Cosmic Chaos	Gloom
Epic Disturbance	Confusion	Dejection Misery
Slap in the Face	Gray, Desolate World	Slammed
Blackest Mood	Dazed	Tumult
		Turmoil

To set the tone use a variety of colors. They are mood injectors that create strong imagery. Colors represent deepest feelings and emotions attached to a stage.

- **White** signifies innocence, purity, and youth.
- **Black** carries darkness, mystery, and trouble.
- **Gray** brings confusion, sadness, and disorientation.
- **Brown** is protection and honesty, and can be blandness.
- **Red** promotes action, passion, and aggression.
- **Yellow** displays optimism, hope, and opening up.
- **Orange** holds balance and energy.
- **Purple** connects to transformation, wisdom, and evolving.

Colors help give stages an identity that tone needs. A gray sky, a red piece of clothing, a painting with an orange background unlock long-repressed memories. Colors open up your unconscious, add realism and depth to scenes, and bring graphic reality to your tone.

Along with tone and color, upheaval and your other scenes need powerful symbols. Symbols are the signs, figures, and images that bring energy and meaning to scenes. Symbolic images open the mind's eye, unlock the unconscious and free secrets the shadow holds. Court had the airport as a symbol of leaving home and Sylvia had a sliding home as a symbol of continuing loss. Pick symbols to represent your upheaval.

Symbols stand in for and clarify the meaning of something else. Their application is situational. They may stand for different things in different scenes. Almost everything can serve as a symbol. It's an object, image or act that represents your thoughts or feelings.

Symbols reveal complex moods, deeper values, and universal truths that invite inner wisdom to come forward. For Sylvia, in the second scene where her house begins to slide down the hill, what better symbol could there be for a life slipping out of control? In scene two Court driving past the McDonald's headquarters is a perfect symbol of his inability to live up to Midwestern family values.

- The symbols are there in your unconscious and they'll appear in unexpected ways and at surprising places.
- They're a reason why it's important to have a journal to jot down symbols the moment they appear.
- Symbols bring focus, reality, and depth to your scenes.
- They never draw a clear line. Instead they nod in one direction.
- Whether your consciousness is aware of it or not, the unconscious stores memories in the form of symbols and when motivated, it adds them to your scene.

Upheaval needs a blend of approaches to depict the effort it takes to deal with the turmoil that has turned your life upside down. Colors and symbols help to show how you're shocked and disoriented. In your confused tone you reveal the extent of the disruption. Symbols bring a deeper meaning to turmoil.

For your upheaval scene to work it needs to use tone, colors, and symbols to express the confusion and surprise, possibly even the anger you're feeling in this second stage of your Cycle Journey Story.

THREE

The Gray Stage, Trauma

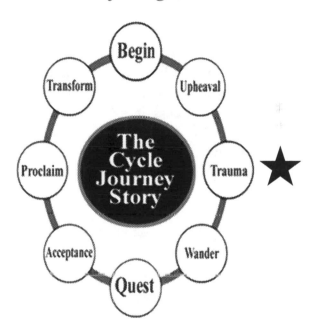

Sorrow in the Dark and the Light
"Truly, it is in the darkness that one finds the light, so when
we are in sorrow, then this light is nearest of all to us."
~Meister Eckhart, German Philosopher

An Introduction To Stage Three

Shout, scream, yell, whisper, you can't verbalize in any of those ways if you don't have a voice. Trauma, stage three, is the aftermath of the upheaval. You're flabbergasted and stunned, in such shock and surprise that you are voiceless. In The Essentials section you'll look at the different aspects of trauma, from the black moods that accompany the bleakness that's overtaken your life to the value of a formal lament.

There are movie examples such as *It's A Wonderful Life* and the *Horse Whisperer* that reveal trauma has long been a subject of interest in our culture. The Deeper Insight delves into the entire psyche, the Self. Then it's back to story time. Humpty Dumpty is still shocked and puzzled over his great fall and our stories show us reeling and unable to understand why we are experiencing more trauma-filled upheavals.

Stage Three concludes with another Tell * Journal * Write coaching where you'll get guidance on how to add a lament to your trauma scene.

The Essentials

Melancholy is a despondency and dejection of spirit or mind, a deep sadness that creates overpowering sorrow. Trauma attached to upheaval bottles up sorrow and bleakness and produces the overwhelming feeling of desolation that finds a home at the center of a Dark Night.

In most societies to suffer in silence, to be alone with one's sorrow or mournfulness, to tough it out, is considered a virtue and a sign of resolution. This overused adage means trauma's inner pain, the repressed memories which are drawn into your unconscious, are never given a voice.

The gray stage is a choice point in the Cycle Journey. Will you bottle up memories attached to the inner pain deep inside you and let its pressure grow into Dark Night despair and misery or will you find a way to verbalize your grief, sorrow, and regret?

For many a code of self-imposed silence demands that they never reveal a demoralizing black mood has overwhelmed them. Others find a voice to tell the tale of their trauma then move past the chaos, confront the challenges and put their energy into coming up with life-changing solutions. The shared trait in those who move past an upheaval and its internalized Dark Night trauma is finding the power of expression, a voice they can give to their grief, sorrow, and regret.

One way to recognize the gray stage, unvoiced trauma, is to know its symptoms:

- Panic attacks and insomnia.
- Difficulty concentrating.
- Isolation from friends and family.
- Flashbacks and dreams.
- Out-of-control emotions, nightmares, weeping, and anger.
- Not connecting with day-to-day life.

Chaotic feelings not drawn out of the unconscious can surface in fits of rage, which increase numbness, shock, and devastation. Those overpowering, out-of-control emotions often are intense enough to bring on physical illnesses such as headaches, racing heartbeat, unexplained aches and pains, ulcers, and asthma.

Meditation is an excellent approach for calming pressurized, hectic, frenzied, and tumultuous states of mind accompanying trauma. It's a reflective, calmer and more adaptable way of existing in the world, an approach which nurtures a stable, clearer mind and creates internal balance—qualities which can remain dormant when there is no effort to develop them. Meditation, clearing your mind, opens you to deeper messages from your unconscious and inner wisdom, which are needed to give voice to inner pain. (see Review of Literature, Salzberg, Sharon, Real Happiness, The Power of Meditation. 2011)

Once you're calm, a lament can be the first step in finding the trauma voice that allows you to tell your story. Over the centuries and in different situations the lament has given a voice to the grief, sorrow, and regret associated with upheaval. Ancient epics like the Iliad, the Odyssey and Beowulf contain laments. In the Old Testament there is a Book of Lamentations. Operatic laments are in Mozart's Marriage of Figaro and Rossini's Barber of Seville. Famous poets like Percy Bysshe Shelly, William Carlos Williams, and Edna St. Vincent Malay wrote laments. Laments have stayed around because they're a way to give voice to the fear attached to emotional pain.

In Shakespeare's *Richard II* King Richard expressed this lament:

"My grief lies all within,
And these external manners of lament,
Are merely shadows of the unseen grief,
That swells with silence in the tortured soul."

A lament is a personal mantra and an expression of an internal storm of uncontrolled feelings drawn out of the unconscious. Shakespeare had it right when he said "my grief lies all within." The lament's structure encourages your Active Imagination to connect with your unconscious and give voice to painful memories it has repressed.

A lament is **regret** linked to disappointment.
A lament is **sorrow** for what could have been.
A lament is the **grief** over a lost opportunity.

A lament begins with some form of **if only,** a way of expressing regret or saying I wouldn't be feeling despondent if the upheaval hadn't happened. Think of **if only** as an invitation to the unconscious to open up. Then the **pleading** or the core of the lament sets forth your sorrow, what you're despondent about. For the first time inner-trauma can claim its own voice.

Common types of core lament *pleadings* are:

If only - I hadn't gotten fired.
If only - I hadn't gotten divorced.
If only - I hadn't quit school.
If only - I had the right career.

At the end of **if only** and a **pleading** comes a special lament addition which identifies the consequences of the lament's pleading, a **bemoaning,** which expresses the deep grief, disapproval, or the distress the core lament has caused. In other words you mourn the lament.

If only - I hadn't gotten fired, **I wouldn't be losing my home.**
If only - I hadn't gotten divorced, **I wouldn't be lonely.**
If only - I hadn't quit school, **I'd get the promotion.**
If only - I had the right career, **I'd have a meaningful life.**

Look at what's been packed into one lament-**bemoaning** statement. There's **if only,** a **pleading** or core lament and a **bemoaning,** or the consequences attached to the pleading. You've given a strong, well defined voice to the trauma and its sorrow, grief and regret.

To give the lament and **bemoaning** power, it needs to be answered. It takes time for an answer, which already lies in your inner wisdom, to come forward and take hold.

The classic movie *It's A Wonderful Life* has a less stripped down lament. "Oh, Pop, I couldn't stand being cooped up for the rest of my life in a shabby office. Oh, I'm sorry Pop. I didn't mean that, but this business of nickels and dimes and spending all your life trying to figure out how to save three cents on a length of pipe... I'd go crazy. I'd go crazy. I want to do something big and something important."

The sorrow, regret, and fear George Bailey feels about the possibility of being trapped in his hometown of Bedford Falls is unmistakable. It's the last sentence, "I want to do something big and something important." which expresses his core lament. His **full lament and bemoaning** could be stated, "If only I could do something big and something important, my life would have meaning." At the end of the movie, with the help of his guardian angel Clarence, George is able to answer his lament. His life in Bedford Falls and what he means to his family is as big and important as anything he could ever want.

Even though it may not have been in the traditional **if only**, **pleading**, and **bemoaning** form, you may have, like George Bailey, repeated your lament countless times.

- Laments tell of the frustration of an upheaval.
- An organized lament becomes a voice for emotional pain.
- Laments have a structure which help us define the uniqueness of our fears.

Author Nicholas Evans' 1995 novel the *Horse Whisperer* tells the tale of a riding accident and its trauma-filled aftermath. In a collision with a truck Grace's friend Judith and her horse are killed and Grace and her horse, Pilgrim, are badly hurt. Grace, her right leg partially amputated, turns bitter and angry and pulls away from the world. Pilgrim is in such turmoil there's a belief he should be put down. This tale shows how the horse's and girl's emotional pain spreads through her family and reaches into the life of the horse whisperer, Tom Booker, and tells how Grace travels the long and difficult road toward stating and answering her lament.

In Donna Tartt's Pulitzer Prize novel, *The Goldfinch*, after Theo's mother is killed in a terrorist attack. Trauma grabs hold of Theo and never releases him. His emotional anguish brings on crippling self-pity, depression, and fear of death. Everything he does reminds him of his mother. Throughout the rest of the book he is trapped in his regrets and fails to get his life back on track. Unexpressed emotional trauma, as it does with Theo, often strips away the ability to feel there is anything routine or normal in life and leaves its victim constantly on guard, waiting for the next attack. The isolation that accompanies emotional suffering makes it tempting, as it did for Theo, to turn angry and hostile then retreat or pull back from the world, do anything to escape the pain.

Each trauma victim must create their own lament. Individual responses shouldn't be compared. Once a victim learns to voice the lament and comes up with an answer, it's possible to relieve the internal pressure and move past the trauma with its failures, heartbreaks, and fears and grow and change. It's the lament, in whatever form it's stated, which uses Active Imagination, connecting the unconscious and conscious, to crystalize the willpower to pick up the pieces and learn from the trauma.

The lament may come to you in bits and pieces. If you find yourself having trouble creating a satisfactory lament, meditate every time you revise your lament. This simple, ongoing practice supports and enhances connecting the unconscious and conscious. It improves the Active Imagination and its power and efficiency in seeing the full impact of the upheaval get better with an ongoing commitment. Through meditation you become increasingly aware of lament messages from your unconscious and you access your inner wisdom with little effort. Your awareness of the full scope of your upheaval increases. To write an effective lament, begin by meditating to calm an anxious mind and stressed out body.

Notice the lament is a verbal expression that can be refined in your journal and revised in a written scene, but its real power lies in its ability to help you tell your story with passion and belief.

The gray stage is a necessary growth part of the Cycle Journey. It acts as a constant reminder of what's at stake if you don't reach the state of calmness necessary to develop the lament and its bemoaning and give trauma its voice.

Stage 3 Deeper Insight

The Self

"Though we know of the self, yet it is not known. You may see a big town and know its name and geographical position, yet you do not know a single one of its inhabitants. You may even know a man through daily intercourse, yet you can be entirely ignorant of his real character." ~ C. G. Jung's letter to Arvind Vasavada

To understand the Self is the first step in voicing trauma. The Self takes in the entire psyche and its possibilities, including the conscious and unconscious. It is the part of us beyond experience and knowledge and is unchangeable. The Self is the organizing mastermind behind the personality. It functions to bring about the best coming to terms with each stage of the Cycle Journey. The goal of the Self is the wholeness and balance achieved in transformation that leads to individuation.

The Self seeks harmony between the opposing parts of the psyche and is a deep inner guiding element in charge of making the entire psyche work as an integrated whole. Without the emergence of the Self, change is impossible.

As you move toward transformation, the job of the Self is to bring inner wisdom to the surface and blend it into your thoughts, intuitions, feelings, and sensations, making it part of non-repressed memories. It moves you toward expanded awareness and deeper insights you can express at a conscious level. Accessing inner wisdom is the way you expand and deepen your personality and break down the barrier between the inner and outer worlds. Your first step is to find a voice for the inner pain created by an upheaval.

Inner wisdom is a balancing addition to consciousness, adding both depth and flexibility to the way we view the world. Deep knowledge exposes hidden creativity, bottled up imagination, latent intuition, and a voice capable of expressing the trauma that follows an upheaval. Once this inner wisdom is brought into the conscious world, your perception and perspective are enlarged and the Self reaches its full potential.

The next stage where the Self and inner wisdom make an appearance is in the quest. Its guidance is necessary for selecting the quest goal and it maintains the motivation to complete the quest.

In transformation you'll gain confidence in relying on inner wisdom and realize the Self is actively leading you toward wholeness.

The Stories For Stage Three

Humpty's Scene Three:

Raw Emotions

He has terrifying nightmares about falling off the wall, watching his yoke spill into the dirt. He always hears the cruel, self-righteous laughs of his dad and boss.

Court's Scene Three:

Abandoned

"Son of a bitch, she moved out."

Sylvia's Scene Three:

Fallen And Broken

I lay in the snow and tried to push away the red hot, burning pain shooting through my body.

Your Cycle Journey Story:

Scene Three - Trauma

Humpty's Story Continues:
Chapter Three: Raw Emotions

Frightened Humpty doesn't yet realize he's in shock from his terrible tumble. He's depressed. At the same time he's furious and spoiling for a fight and he's not sure why. He quarrels with his wife over nothing and screams at his egglets for the slightest infraction—they run in the other direction whenever they see him coming. To avoid shell-shaking stares from his family and overly sympathetic visitors, he spends most of his day locked in the bedroom, only coming out when he's wrapped in his prized brown fleece cozy blanket.

Some nights he sneaks down to the kitchen and sits in the dark, his cozy blanket wrapped tightly around his shell, drinking cup after cup of spiced pumpkin cider. Other evenings he compulsively runs his hands over his damaged outer surface. It's not unusual for Humpty to stare out the window as he laments his fate and searches for a way to go back to his old life. He has terrifying nightmares where he falls off the wall, sits on the ground and watches his yoke form a small yellow river in the dirt. In the distance he hears the cruel, self-righteous laughs of his dad and boss.

Yesterday his youngest egglet, Doodle, came home crying inconsolably. Between sobs she blurted out, "At recess my best friends Fiddle and Piddle wouldn't stop making fun of your missing pieces and cracks. Dad, don't you see, I can't listen to them mock my father?"

Humpty burst into tears.

A few hours later he's at the Egg On Your Face Tavern in a booth in the darkest corner. His brown cozy blanket is pulled around his mutilated shell. Humpty, desperate for outside advice, is meeting his best friend, a turtle egg, Bob Easter, who worked with him at the hatchery.

To avoid Bob's look of pity, he keeps his eyes on the table top and speaks barely above a whisper. "There are days my great fall feels like too much of an ordeal to stand. I'm confused. Nothing makes sense. It's gotten so bad I've lost interest in my favorite pastime, reading Mother Goose nursery rhymes to the egglets."

Bob scratches his shell and looks away. "My friend, I don't mean to be unkind. Perhaps you should consider what other eggs with badly damaged shells have done—climb over the wall, go into the dark woods and disappear for good."

Bob stands and backs away from the table. "One more thing old friend, I could lose my job if anyone sees us together. We must never meet again." Without looking back, Bob heads for the door.

Humpty admits he's an outcast. His life is so scrambled he sees himself as mutilated to the point where he no longer feels like a true egg. What's worse he can't think of any way to get his old life back. After years as the example of shell perfection, he admits he's turned into a horrid aberration every normal egg wishes would climb over the wall and disappear in the dark forest. He becomes desperate enough to visit the carton of a duck egg, Honker, who several months ago had a great fall of his own.

This mystifyingly jovial egg, jagged cracks and missing pieces covering a shell dyed with bright reds and yellows, invites Humpty into a living room where crumpled drawing paper litters the floor.

Humpty stares. Honker laughs. "Dumpty, don't you get it? I don't have time to fixate on my appearance."

The disfigured egg looks out to the three-story apartment coop across the street, gives Humpty a hard stare and blurts out a wakeup call. "Your cracks aren't any worse than mine. I say it's time for you to take off that silly blanket and get on with life."

Can't Honker see he's an unsightly mess? How can any self-respecting egg be so casual about a devastating defacement that invites ridicule from the entire egg kingdom?

Honker reaches behind the couch and pulls out a large sketch pad. He flips through the pages and shows Humpty portraits of young goose eggs. "Dumpty, the cracks were a watershed moment. Today I have an exciting career as an artist. I've promised myself to make a sketch of every newly laid egg in my flock and present my portrait to the mother goose. This passion for drawing takes up all my time. Already there's so much demand for my egg likenesses that for months I haven't had a chance to think about these cracks."

Humpty stares. How can Honker ignore his ghastly shell and get past everyone pointing at his flaws? Sketches of goose eggs sounds ridiculous. Silly drawings won't change anything. Can't Honker see he's a mutilated shell, an object of pity who needs a blanket of his own? Even surgery at the hatchery clinic won't repair his damage.

Humpty doesn't care about mindless diversions, like doing sketches of newly born goose eggs. Still wrapped in his cozy blanket, he walks away from Honker's carton and for the first time states his lament, "If only I hadn't fallen, I'd still have my over-easy life."

With no answer for the mourning of his pre-fall life, hopelessness sets in. Humpty's grief overcomes him. He heads home in the grip of the blackest mood he's ever experienced.

A few blocks from the carton, from high up in an ancient oak, he hears the sharp, cawing voice of a crow. "You, the mutilated egg, I've heard about your revolting appearance."

Humpty looks up as a crow as dark as the darkest night and its great black wings spread, circles the oak twice as it floats to the ground. The blue-black bird looking like it had been personally crafted by the forest darkness, nods its head to the left and to the right then shakes its knife-like beak. "I'm Basil the witch's ambassador sent to the egg kingdom to see if the rumors about your cracks and missing pieces were true. That awful shell, it's no wonder you have to cover yourself."

"I fell off the wall." Humpty wipes a tear from his eye.

Basil flaps his wings. "The day we lured you into the dark forest there would be great celebration when we boiled you in the witch's kettle. You could have become a legend the foxes and crows talked about for centuries. After your tumble, one look at your shell would turn even the foulest forest creature's stomach. Stay with your own kind, we want nothing to do with such a loathsome egg."

Court's Scene Three

Abandoned

I found a home just outside of L. A. on one of the remote beaches in Oxnard, California. An English girl, who I was attracted to mostly for her accent, and I had a cottage a half-block from the beach. I worked enough to pay the bills and spent the rest of my time at a local neighborhood bar with a great ocean view. It all seemed close to ideal until the day I came home, opened the door and got a whiff of that dead smell that goes with an empty house.

"No chairs, no couch, no rugs, no TV, no lamps, just my painting sitting above hooks and nails scattered along the fireplace mantle." It didn't take any brain power to tell my relationship prospects had taken another sharp downward turn.

I looked about the living room and stared at the only thing left, my painting of a somber, barn-like dwelling in a black frame. The home in the middle of a dark field with a stream of light shining out an open door symbolized my abandoned feeling.

A dusty odor, like every particle of dirt had been stirred up, made me take a step back. I struggled to take in the chilling emptiness. In near darkness and total confusion I stayed statue still.

"Son of a bitch, she moved out." My voice echoed through the empty house.

Except for my office, the rest of the gray-tiled cottage didn't have a speck of furniture. Beds gone, empty cupboards, even the shower curtains taken down, a numb, paralyzed feeling took hold. Maybe there'd be a flash and everything would return to normal.

In my office, the second bedroom, I turned on the single light and stared at the only furniture she'd left, my desk, chair, and bookcase. The desolate, alone sensation I'd had when my marriage ended returned. I'd been transported back to where I started. I felt like a department store dummy without the brains to learn the most basic lessons.

I repeated the oath. "Son of a bitch." What else could I say?

Okay, our relationship had been turning sour for months—a mismatch at a cosmic level. More irritating she wanted me to get a responsible job, earn enough money to buy a house and get married. I wasn't ready for a major commitment. Still moving out when I was gone for the day went beyond a bombshell. I made a half-hearted attempt to collect my thoughts, but didn't have a clue what to do next. A wave of paralyzing panic hit. I had to think of something.

By now the sun had set and the house felt eerie, almost haunted. At this point of desperation I would have welcomed the company of a friendly ghost.

That's when I had this weird out-of-body experience, like I could look down on myself. Any kind of relationship which included responsibility or long-term promises scared me silly. I'd do almost anything to avoid another emotional trauma like my divorce.

The funny thing is that by doing my best to avoid getting close I'd created the same abandoned feeling I had when I left Chicago.

Maybe we were two people with commitment phobias. I should do something, go somewhere and take action, but what and where? I could call her every nasty name I could think of—reality check, in an empty house who'd care. Some little boy part of me wanted to cry—I wouldn't descend into whiny emotion.

A soul-weary heaviness welled up. Without changing my clothes I got out of the desk chair, laid on the floor, curled up into a fetal position and went to sleep. The next morning, Saturday, I opened my eyes and looked around the empty house. A note on the kitchen shelf scribbled with a red marker read, "You're a no good, worthless sod and we're through. I detest you."

Her no holds barred declaration gave me one of those moments of clarity. It's possible for two intense emotions to exist at the same time. A big part of me wanted her gone. I didn't have to try and make a difficult relationship work. I felt relieved. Another section of my numbed brain wallowed in guilt and self-pity. I'd been divorced, one failed relationship. This time I'd been abandoned. My second botched try at love pointed to an undeniable conclusion that I didn't have what it took to be relationship material. Maybe I should have stuck with my original idea and gotten a dog.

For the first time I faced an unpleasant truth I'd done my best to keep deep inside. No matter how much I lamented, I did everything possible to destroy my marriage and I hadn't done anything to support this relationship. Instead I stayed distant and wary. I'd never gotten around protecting myself. I could have been the poster boy for seeing the glass as half empty.

Sometime around noon I got hungry and went out to get a hamburger. I stuffed the burger and fries in my mouth. My churning stomach told me I would have been better off staying hungry. Maybe a drink would calm me down. One sip of the vodka and tonic and I knew liquor would only bring on more self-pity.

I drove around for a while, which seemed aimless. I took a walk on the beach and couldn't take in the beauty. After a couple of minutes at the mall, I knew I didn't want to be around people. Defeated at every attempt to distract my emotions and feeling a little like a movie psycho, I went home, sunk down in the desk chair and stared at the wall for the rest of the afternoon.

Sunday morning I went to a bookstore, but couldn't concentrate enough to open a book. I shot pool and got suspicious ax murder glances when I kept banging the balls into each other. In a state of absolute confusion and desperation, I tried bowling and must have set a record for gutter balls.

Monday, as if some part of the dark cloud unexpectedly lifted, I felt better. A dreadful weekend in a nearly empty house taught me emotional trauma is real, a wound that needs time to heal. The inner pain is anchored in not being able to give voice to your overwhelming mood swings. No amount of willpower drives those feelings away. They leave when they're ready. The best comparison I can make is it's like someone beat you up, left you in a dark alley black and blue with bleeding cuts and scratches.

Take it from me, without giving your pain a voice it's a dark, paralyzing hurricane-like frame of mind you can't avoid or ignore, and it's even worse when you're home alone.

I had to find a way to lament my frustrations and fears and answer how I'd deal with the choking grip a self-protective attitude had on my life. The message I got from the empty house is, at least for a while, I needed to stay away from long-term relationships. If I didn't have any responsibility, I wouldn't have another failed relationship. Until I found a new way to look at my life I'd avoid commitment like it was a plague.

STITCHING – Connecting Scenes Three and Four:

I'm naive about what makes relationships work. After the home alone event I said "what the hell." Nothing in my life worked and I didn't have a clue how to make the necessary changes.

That's when an inspiration hit. I could go with the flow, take whatever jobs came up and date a lot, but never getting so serious I'd have to commit to anyone.

My drive vanished along with my marriage. On a conscious level I felt relieved, but deeper down I sensed I was frightened. A couple of months later I'd found a new apartment on an even more remote beach and decided, as long as it was different I'd take just about any job.

Sylvia's Scene Three

Fallen and Broken

Alone on the mountain I hit an icy spot and fell. My boot binding didn't release. I lay in the snow and tried to push away the burning pain. Somewhere in the distance there were shouts. I'd say anything and promise anything if whoever came for me could make this agony stop.

My senses recoiled at the antiseptic hospital smell. I opened an eye and peeked out. The dark-haired, white-coated man at my bedside had the corners of his mouth turned down. He shook his head and gave the kind of impatient clinical stare an engineer gets when he can't wait to get his hands on a broken machine.

I moaned. He ignored me and cleared his throat. "Sylvia this is no time for beating around the bush. Your lower leg and ankle are crushed, here's the best way to fix them."

He cleared his throat again and leaned closer. "I'll drill a hole through your heel bone, hang weights from it and put a sling under your left leg." His voice got soft. "Here's the sticky part, you'll be forced to lay on your back and not move until we see if healing starts. Once that happens I'll put on a special cast."

He took a breath and looked down at the chart in his hand and did his best to look positive. "Bottom line, there's no time to waste. You need to make a decision on my treatment plan right now."

In a quiet voice the surgeon explained only a few months ago he'd returned from Europe where he learned a new technique for working with my type of injury. He waved his black pen over my leg and in an excited voice went into detail. "If I follow standard procedure and put a cast on now, you'll have one short leg."

Again he held his pen over my ankle and gestured. "Right now it's like jelly inside your ankle. Without my treatment there's no way to keep your leg from getting shorter. If my treatment doesn't work, you'll limp and have to wear a built-up shoe for the rest of your life."

I felt helpless, more like terrified. If the treatment worked, I'd have to stay in the hospital and be imprisoned in a cast for who knows how long. If it didn't I'd have one leg shorter than the other. The decision to go skiing felt like the most reckless thing I'd ever done.

That trauma-filled scene had its roots in our home loss the previous winter. I'd handled the stress the best I could, at least until months later when my hands broke out in horrible itching blisters.

The bills kept piling up and I had to work every possible hour. By layering cotton gloves under rubber gloves while I used shampoo, dyes, and permanent wave solutions, I managed to stay at my salon. Every day the blisters got worse. At night the burning and itching made it feel like my hands were on fire. Soaking my hands in vinegar seemed to be the only thing that helped. My girls complained their mother smelled like a pickle.

Nothing did any good. I absorbed enough toxic chemicals to end up with blood poisoning, had to stop working, couldn't sell the salon and finally turned it over to my top hairdresser.

By now we'd moved into in a partially completed house we were building ourselves. We lived a few miles from a huge ski resort where I found a job as a cashier at the food counter.

The night before the accident a gentle, fluffy snow fell. The next morning the sun glistened off snow-laden tree branches. I didn't have to work and my younger daughter and I couldn't wait to go skiing. At the resort my daughter headed to her ski school. I took the chair lift up to one of the higher slopes and started down.

Maybe the sliding house had been a warning I needed to stay off hills, anyway that fateful decision changed my life. It couldn't have been more than a few hundred yards from the top when the ski hit an icy patch and I went down. The ski boot binding didn't release. Unbelievable searing pain shot up my left leg. I screamed for help and vaguely remember someone calling for the ski patrol. They lifted me into their sled, fixed a splint around my boot, took me to the lodge and called Jake.

He came in the station wagon. The panicked look on his face told me I was in serious trouble. He decided, rather than wait for an ambulance, it would be faster to take me down the hill to the city hospital emergency room.

With one hand gripping the steering wheel and the other beating on the horn, it took over a half hour to drive down the winding mountain road. By the time we got to the hospital I was screaming, wailing, and crying, and going into severe shock. Within seconds the emergency room crew put me on a gurney and gave me a knockout shot.

After the surgery, for the next month, as we waited for my ankle to begin to heal, the hospital bed and room became my world. The slightest twist or turn put my leg in agony. It felt like medieval torture to lay on my back, not moving, except when absolutely necessary, which usually caused more pain. Somehow, between pain pills and relying on my own meditative abilities, with bed sores and all the rest, I made it through the worst ordeal of my life.

Again and again I've gone over each **if only**. **If only** I hadn't gotten divorced, **if only** I hadn't moved to the mountains with the bad weather and all its problems, **if only** I hadn't gotten blood poisoning and had to take the job at the ski resort and most of all, **if only** I hadn't gone skiing that day, I wouldn't be in this mess and feeling like I might be a cripple for the rest of my life. I had way too much fear from way too many **if only** laments and not nearly enough answers.

At the end of thirty days my leg healed enough for my surgeon to mold a plaster cast around my ankle, leg and up to my hip. The day he put on the cast is burned into my memory. He told me, "No pain meds Sylvia. I need you to be awake and aware enough to tell me by the feel if the bones are in the right place." I gritted my teeth and worked with the doctor. Like he was creating a sculpture, layer by wet layer the plaster cast went on. I never knew time could pass so slowly.

I still recall the overwhelming gratitude I felt for the family, friends, nurses, and doctors. My one regret is I'd gotten so absorbed in my own healing I'm not sure I said thank you to all the people who helped me and the family. On New Year's Eve, in the best late Christmas present ever, with my leg propped up, they wheeled me out of the hospital. The same volunteer fire department friends who helped when we lost our mountain house carried me through a snow storm to our home. A year later my ankle and leg had healed and my left leg ended up the same length as my right. It took several months of physical therapy before I learned to walk again.

I knew what it meant to be tested. From one winter through the next, I'd lost my home, business, and my physical ability. I had one of those stunning insights. Could it be the storm of turmoil from the sliding house and the broken leg were connected, a defining point in life? The first tragedy made the second worse and the first trauma made the second more devastating. Their connection had a sobering effect. I couldn't live through another winter in the mountains, especially since due to a building moratorium, Jake and I didn't have jobs. In the late summer we sold our newly built house, moved back to the city and started over. I realized I could let this turmoil ruin my life or I could see it as an opportunity to begin again.

Over time I've had my ankle fused, and my knee and hip replaced. My walking ability is limited, but I feel grateful I have a leg, can walk and manage the pain. The effects of that emotional trauma still impact me. It's hard for me to express the sorrow I feel over so many mishaps. Loss is the theme running through my life. I'd been forced out of my grandparent's home and I'd lost the house where I thought I could build a happy family. The shattered ankle represented a loss of personal safety. The fear I would never be safe continued to build. I felt myself pulling back and becoming more protective.

STITCHING – <u>Connecting Scenes Three and Four:</u>

The shattered ankle taught me I'm a survivor. I'm thankful my wonderful doctor had the skill to keep me from being a cripple for life. I discovered life is fragile and you're never more than a step away from your world unraveling before your eyes. A sliding house, a shattered leg, multiple broken relationships and unemployed, how could I squeeze so much drama into one life? What's wrong with me and what's next? The thought that I'd somehow been jinxed plagued me.

Tell * Journal * Write

Scene Three

As coaches and teachers we know one of the hardest trauma challenges is finding your voice. That's where this scene helps the most. You can Tell * Journal* Write until you've captured the traumatic effect of the Dark Night.

At the beginning of Humpty's chapter three he is frightened, in shock, and depressed. He has bottled-up his **regret, sorrow, and grief** and has no way to voice his feelings.

> **Regret** is the remorse you feel for the turmoil the upheaval brought into your life. It's a deep personal dissatisfaction over the Dark Night. Before you start your scene list what you regret. It could be the loss of a loved one or an accident that limits physical activity or any major loss in your life.
>
> **Sorrow** is the distress caused by the loss or disappointment accompanying the upheaval. Sorrow is the glue holding the Dark Night together. It forms the voice for your grief and might show itself in loneliness or in heartbreak.
>
> **Grief** is the inner pain of upheaval turmoil and the foundation of your mourning. Unhappiness, heartache and misery are a swirl of grief emotions that form a pleading wail for escaping your Dark Night.

In a trauma scene, identify specific ways your regret, sorrow, and grief make themselves known. Are you not sleeping? Do you have bouts of weeping? Have you lost your temper over a trivial incident? Once you've confronted your regret, sorrow, and grief and answered the lament you've given trauma the voice it needs.

The **core sentence's job is to** anchor the trauma scene voice. Court's scene has this sentence near the beginning, "No chairs, no couch, no rugs, no TV, no lamps, just that painting sitting above hooks and nails scattered along the fireplace mantle. It wasn't hard to tell my relationship prospects had taken another sharp downward turn." The dark, despondent tone of abandonment and aloneness set up the rest of the scene. His stark word choice makes his fear and confusion evident.

Once the core sentence is in place give depth and purpose to your trauma voice by adding the **lament and bemoaning statement**. This is a critical part of scene three. It's the pronouncement that shows you understand the costs of the upheaval.

With the core sentence and lament in place, for the first time you have a clear voice. Now complete your scene. Don't analyze. Work with your emotions and let your unconscious pull up the melancholy feelings. When Court developed scene three he imagined himself back in his empty house, felt the loneliness, confusion and anger, and used the hurt voice for the rest of the scene. For the third scene Sylvia had to recall her pain and alarm she would be permanently disabled and let a panicked voice express her fear.

Is the voice in your trauma scene angry, fearful or confused? What does a trauma voice sound like? It could be barely above a whisper or it could stammer out words. Maybe there are long gaps of silence between its sentences. Use similes to establish a comparison. To Court the voice in his head raged like an angry storm.

Shorter sentences reveal trauma tension. Don't go into long explanations. The trauma voice is rooted in your feelings and emotions. Are you mournful or heartsick? The trauma voice might tell of not sleeping or not being able to eat a favorite meal. Read the scene out loud. Get used to the way the voice sounds. See if it represents the way you feel or felt after the upheaval.

Trauma and upheaval take place at almost the same time. The **tension, conflict and fear** from an upheaval should be unmistakable in your trauma voice. Your scene needs to reveal growing **fear** that everything has spun out of control. You may feel at war with yourself and that mysterious, uncontrollable forces have arisen to oppose your interests or principles. Show an awareness this escalating **conflict** needs to be resolved.

A byproduct of conflict and fear is unrelenting mental strain and anxiety. You lead a **tension**-filled life. Upheaval has initiated the conflict, tension, and fear mix. In trauma the mix reaches a storm-like high point as you search for a voice to express inner pain.

Words which help guide the trauma scene are:

Turmoil	Uproar	Resentment
Disorder	Grief	Heartsick
Confusion	Tumult	Chaos
Unrest	Anger	Confusio

Try to view the trauma scene as not being isolated. How does it affect your entire Cycle Journey Story? Court voiced his trauma lesson by deciding he didn't want commitments where he'd have another failed relationship and he'd take whatever job came along so he wouldn't have the pressure of a career. After her sliding house in the mountains and shattered ankle from the ski accident, Sylvia feared another devastating blow could come at any moment, pulled back and became more protective. Those decisions propelled them into the wandering stage.

When you complete your scene, add a last paragraph that makes clear what deeper insights and expanded awareness you gained by finding your trauma voice.

FOUR

The Brown Stage, Wandering

Alone and Searching for Light "So we follow our wandering paths, and the very darkness acts as our guide and our doubts serve to reassure us."

~Jean-Pierre de Cassade – Jesuit Priest

An Introduction To Stage Four

Think of yourself as lost in a desert or a giant forest with no way back to civilization. That's what wandering, stage four, feels like. There's an upside, a positive way to look at your situation. You're free, maybe for the first time to look for a new life path.

In The Essentials there are different looks at what it means to wander and a warning that it's possible to get trapped in wandering. Old classics like *Alice In Wonderland*, an edgy book, *The Long Dark Tea-Time of the Soul*, and a newer bestseller, *Wild*, illustrate how differently wandering can be experienced. Active Imagination as a Deeper Insight points to bridging the unconscious and the conscious to find a way out of wandering. Humpty Dumpty admits he's been shaken to the core and wants to recover from his great fall. Our stories show us still struggling to find new meaning for our lives.

Stage Four Tell * Journal * Write coaching focuses on how to build backstory and turning point moments.

The Essentials

Do you remember the Lost Boys in Peter Pan and Never Land? Wandering is that kind of time out of time, a reality which is part hideout, part escape, and part of a necessary breakaway to allow you to find a new direction and get in touch with the person you were always meant to be. It can be a safe haven, a place to take chances and try things. In a sense wandering has the intent of drifting to find direction.

Wandering's danger lies in your new direction being elusive or undiscoverable. Be careful. Stay too long in the world of wanderers, ramble too much, roam too long or drift too far and like the Lost Boys you'll be in danger of being drawn into a permanent hollowness, a mist-filled alternative existence with no way to escape and undertake a quest for an authentic destiny.

You are on an aimless nomadic exploration without form, substance, or purpose. There is a sense of life turning into an endless time in the wilderness. Rootlessness brings on choking boredom where every day lacks direction. It's a year-after-year recycling which is over here then back over there with no apparent plan or purpose and the unbearable feeling the Dark Night can never be escaped. You become an eternal wanderer, an outlier engaged in an aimless pursuit without a clear sense of what's being chased. Nothing will make sense in this jerky, roving meandering with a never-ending hunt for an unattainable life objective.

There's a possible positive side to wandering. You have an opportunity to disconnect from an old life before embracing a new direction and beginning the search for a new destiny. This is the view of the Cycle Journey wanderer passing through a stage on the way to selecting a quest. Minimum expectations mean there is room to experiment, to try new things, experience new realities with no obvious connection to an old life. This is a chance to take a second look at passions and plans and see youthful dreams from an adult vantage point. Maybe there's a job, career or skill which didn't seem practical.

For the first time there's the freedom to take a second serious look at what appeared to be dreams or unfillable aspirations.

The question is how does the Cycle Journey wanderer spend the time in the void to acquire a new direction? An answer lies in the wanderer's ability to develop a connection between the conscious and the unconscious, to join the inner and outer worlds. Without this link inner world messages won't get through.

Being in a void between worlds is the theme of *The Long Dark Tea-Time of the Soul,* a fantasy detective novel by Douglas Adams. The novel is a quirky look at a world where Norse gods were created by our desire for them. In the modern, cynical world these powerful beings have fallen on hard times. Thor, the thunder god, is hanging around Heathrow Airport doing his best to get on a plane to Oslo. Odin, the chief deity, has traded his magical powers to be a one-eyed gentleman who lives in a luxury research hospital where he gets plenty of sleep and has access to clean linen sheets. The other gods, even though they are no longer worshipped don't disappear, but remain on earth as destitute tramps existing in a world parallel to ours, one where London's St. Pancara Railway Station is Valhalla in disguise.

The image of once powerful gods living such an aimless existence captures the pathos of wandering. The new god, Guilt, ends the god's time in the wilderness and shows even gods have to adapt to a modern world. The uncertainty of wandering is expressed by this quote from the book, "I may not have gone where I intended to go, but I think I have ended up where I needed to be."

No book has ever portrayed the mindlessness of wandering better than *Alice's Adventures in Wonderland and Through the Looking Glass.* The fall down the rabbit hole turns Alice's world on its end. She's in a land of twisted logic and absurd conclusions and has to trust she will be able to use her reasoning to make some sense out of nonsense. In the end Alice learns the way out of wandering is to trust herself and her own inner wisdom to take away the nonsense she confronts at the bottom of the rabbit hole.

One of the best contemporary books with a wandering theme is *Wild* by Cheryl Strayed. At twenty-two, four years after her mother's death and a failed marriage she found her direction by hiking alone a thousand miles on the Pacific Crest Trail, from the Mojave Desert through California and Oregon to Washington State. The definition of strayed she used, "to wander from the proper path, to deviate from the direct course, to be lost, to become wild, to be without a mother or father, to be without a home, to move about aimlessly in search of something, to diverge or digress," captures the essence of wandering.

Eternal drifters like the Norse gods are in shock, prisoners of gray, mist-filled worlds where escape is difficult, if not impossible. On the other hand, the passing sightseers like Alice have entered a void forming a necessary separation needed to let go of the earlier dictates. They use the time in wandering to search for a quest that establishes a new life path or makes a course correction. Still others, like Cheryl Strayed, need time in wandering to heal from overwhelming trauma before they select a quest that refocuses their life.

Even for the Cycle Journey wanderer, the common temptation is to repeat old patterns and expect different results. For the first time there's a call to look inward, to figure out where to go after the great fall. The poem, the Cherubimic Wanderer by Angehus Silesius nails the challenge of taking control of wandering.

"By thy own Will thou'rt lost, by thy own Will thou'rt found, Thou by thy Will art freed, and by thy Will art bound."

To paraphrase Silesius, how the journey is made is up to the traveler. To not be drawn into eternal wandering requires the willpower to initiate deliberate action. For the Cycle Journey wanderer, strength of will points the way out of wandering and to the freedom to embrace a new life path and authentic destiny.

Wandering presents a unique opportunity to question what an innermost life free of guilt and open to trust and a feeling of gratitude would be like. Coming out of wandering is a transition point for surrendering to a higher purpose in life.

The psychologist, scholar and author of the New York Times Best Seller, *The Soul's Code,* James Hillman's quote speaks about life purpose. "...the call may have been like gentle pushing in the stream in which you drifted unknowingly to a particular spot on the bank. Looking back, you sense that fate had a hand in it."

It's a truism, a self-evident statement a distinctive life path waits for each of us. Our actions take us away from our calling or lead us to it. When we let go of earlier life restraints, wandering becomes free-wheeling, a pause with time for musing about what's possible internally and externally and coming up with an insightful inspiration for a quest.

We've learned the beginning, upheaval, trauma, and wandering are the necessary foundation for a quest and for continuing a Cycle Journey of change. The first connection between the unconscious and the conscious has been made and there's a growing awareness of the power of repressed memories. What's more we've discovered wandering creates a necessary separation between what brought on the Dark Night and beginning a quest to claim a new life path.

Stage 4 Deeper Insight

Active Imagination

"It was during Advent of the year 1913 – December 12, to be exact – that I resolved the decisive step. I was sitting at my desk once more, thinking over my fears. Then I let myself drop. Suddenly it was as though the ground literally gave way beneath my feet, and I plunged into the dark depths." ~C. G, Jung on Active Imagination

Active imagination is a gateway to freedom from wandering. It's a concept Jung developed that creates a bridge between the conscious and the unconscious and accesses material related to working with dreams and the creative Self through imagination or fantasy. In the Humpty Dumpty Principle it amplifies and shapes written scenes and introduces a dynamic quality into building associations from a small core sentence or phrase. In addition to its key role in scene writing, Active Imagination is behind the trauma scene's lament and bemoaning and plays a critical role in creating a dialogue between the inner critic and inner advocate in acceptance and proclaiming stages.

It places you at a threshold between everyday experience and the unconscious world of creativity and imagination and allows you to use what arises out of this viewpoint in your scenes.

An Active Imagination partnership of the inner world and the outer world results in deeper insights, expanded awareness, focused emotion, and more profound meaning for everyday events.

It has elements of meditation, contemplation, and hypnosis, but Active Imagination is not comparable to any of the three individually. Rather it is a combination of sharpening the mind's reasoning skills and turning off the alert mind. This state of mind allows you to plunge unafraid into the dark depths of the unconscious.

While you are listening to stories, staring at a beautiful view or simply lying in bed in a state between sleep and wakefulness, Active Imagination occurs naturally. James Hillman, the author of the Soul's Code, believes the unconscious is natural and organic and Active Imagination is not done to silence the mind, but to give it greater speech and help us see the mythic and poetic possibilities in the world.

Active Imagination builds an inner outer world bridge with personal symbols and vivid comparisons. This connection creates the unconscious link which expands the consciousness, deepens perception, and makes moving from stage to stage possible.

The Stories For Stage Four

New Potential

Maybe, if he's willing to make the effort, Humpty
realizes he can rise above everyone's limiting
expectations and become more than a beaten egg.

Court's Scene Four:

Jobs Jumble

"What have you done in recent years?"

Sylvia's Scene Four:

Four Divorces

Marriage four where I thought I'd finally been rewarded
for surviving my past divorces still hurts the most.

Your Cycle Journey Story:

Scene Four - Wandering

Humpty's Story Continues:
Chapter Four: New Potential

"Fate has betrayed me. Life has no meaning. Everything I've done is worthless. I'm adrift, confused, and bewildered. If only I hadn't suffered this great fall, my world wouldn't be in such an absolute muddle." Over and over, at the beginning of each day Humpty mumbles his depressed lament.

Each morning, possessed by a clear intention to get back to work, he puts on his frock coat and heads for the front door. The instant his hand brushes against the egg-shaped handle he freezes up and runs back to his bedroom. Day after day he tries, but there is nothing he can do to make himself return to the hatchery and face the ridicule his horrid appearance would invite. After several months of not being able to confront his shame, he quits his once promising hatchery job.

His parents are worried sick and his father, a retired butler at the king's castle, tells Humpty, "Son it's as plain as your disgusting shell, you've lost the thread of life and there's no hope. Your get-up-and-go is gone and you've laid an egg with your family and career."

Before Humpty can recover from the bleak judgement, his wife, Mrs. Dumpty, tears running down her shell, puts a stack of bills, all with past due stamped in red, in his hand. "Husband dear, we are facing a moment of truth. Our savings are gone and our neighbors the Yokemans made no bones about telling me your shocking appearance is a neighborhood blight that's lowering carton property values."

The pressure is too much. Humpty runs back in his bedroom. More days, weeks, and months go by with the listless, miserable Humpty sitting around the house wrapped in his cozy fleece blanket and refusing to let non-family members see what he looks like.

Nothing stirs his interest. He feels shunned and confined. With no way in sight to end his trials, to get out of the house and escape the constant complaining, Humpty, his brown cozy blanket making him look like a monk egg, takes long walks through different parts of the egg kingdom. The diversity stuns him. There are dark basements full of snake eggs and around ponds turtle eggs lie under golden sand. He feels angry no one ever told him about the incredible variety in the kingdom. For the first time he sees greenish lizard eggs and neatly stacked piles of tortoise eggs. His sense of being small and insignificant grows, and yet, for the first time, he understands the almost infinite possibilities his egg universe offers. It amazes him no one pays attention to his cozy blanket or points at his disfigurement.

One night Humpty has a stunning insight. "My great fall has shaken me to the core." His voice quivers. He looks down and pats a crack. "This is a critical point where action must be taken. It's up to me to make sense of it all and discover a new purpose for my life."

The next morning he goes to a spa next to the castle. There he has his 7,000 pores cleansed in spiced tea and his yoke shaken by a team of chanting monk eggs trained in ovum therapy.

That night in the kitchen as he stares into his cup of pumpkin cider a revelation hits. He throws off his blanket and looks down at his cracks and missing pieces. "What's done is done, there's no magical way I'll be able to put myself back together. Life is my adventure and I'm the one who needs to find the courage to change from the inside out. If I'm ever going to become a good egg, one who's real and alive, I have to come up with a new way to look at myself."

Maybe, if he's willing to make the effort, Humpty realizes he can rise above everyone's limiting expectations and become more than a beaten egg. Honker found a new purpose with his sketches. Perhaps Humpty needs a cause too, one which stirs enough true passion to reinvigorate the proteins in his yoke.

That night he has the strangest dream of his life. He's back at his last year of egglet summer camp where he'd been picked as a senior leader who egged on the younger eggs in games and crafts. Those months, a time he never wanted to end, had been the happiest of his life. The most puzzling part of the dream is that none of the campers appeared to notice his shell had missing pieces and cracks. Even stranger, he seemed not to care how he looked.

Humpty wakes and feels his yoke bubble. He recognizes this is his moment of truth, a kind of high noon where he has a chance to make real changes. He rushes to the kitchen table and starts writing about everything that's happened to him, how he feels about the cracks and missing pieces and the advice he's gotten from everyone, including Honker. Next he scribbles down what he remembers from his childhood, especially the first time his mother and father told him shell appearance is everything. For the rest of the day Humpty edits and revises what he's written, begins to see patterns emerge and becomes aware of a possible way to bring new purpose to his life.

Court's Scene Four

Jobs Jumble

I'd moved to Santa Barbara and fallen in love with the city. The town couldn't have been more different than where I grew up—no factories, no taverns and only one up-scale bowling alley. Everyone appeared successful and laid back at the same time. It seemed like there were more writers and artists than in all of the Midwest. I'd found a new hometown.

On a coffee date I learned having eleven jobs in four years isn't an attractive discussion topic. Constance, a successful magazine publisher, asked a casual question. "What have you done in recent years?" She unbuttoned her gold coat and adjusted her designer glasses.

My dark French roast sat on a small table near the brick wall covered with colorful names of the makers of exotic foreign coffees. "I returned to California and a friend from college put me in touch with a "B" list Hollywood actress. She needed someone to make her memoir readable. We met for coffee beside the pool of her Malibu home. She took her manuscript out of a fancy jewelry box and handed it to me—it was handwritten on pink stationary that smelled like roses. By the end of the first page I decided, as impossible as it appeared, her overly dramatic writing showed less promise than her acting. Two agonizing months later I'd finished a publishable version so devoid of truth it could have masqueraded as a cheap romance novel.

Constance stared at me. "You're a good writer. Why use your talents in such a silly way? Maybe you're making this up."

I shook my head. "Total truth, besides she paid great." We were at a local coffeehouse called The Blended Brew, located in an old warehouse a couple of blocks from the ocean.

"Three months after my Hollywood stint, for a half year I had an eye-opening experience as a babysitter for a billionaire's incredibly spoiled daughters and their kids. Take it from me the rich are different and not in a good way."

Constance scooted her chair closer and giggled when I told her about the kids with clothes closets bigger than my apartment.

"After my sitter stint, I sold cellular phones, mostly to surfers who financed riding the waves by being marijuana dealers. One, Benny the Board, had a nasty run-in with the police and I figured a few phone commissions weren't worth the risk."

"You have to be making this up." Her face contorted into a confused, slightly frightened look. "We could turn this into a true life piece for my magazine."

The avant-garde painters, actors between L.A. jobs, aspiring writers and other rolling stones at nearby tables created the picture-perfect backdrop for telling my freewheeling employment history to a very proper looking business woman.

Constance's fingers tapped the tabletop. "Is there more?"

My date, like she wasn't sure what to expect next, snuck a concerned look out of the corner of her eye. I didn't hold back. "Soon after the surfers and I went our separate ways, I wrote a novel about Rasputin and his eerie hypnotic power. The title, *Eyes of the Fire*, ended up being the best thing about the book. I've never let anyone look at it."

"Maybe you should have stuck with rewriting Hollywood autobiographies." Constance looked toward the exit sign. "I'm almost afraid to ask what you did next."

"A few months later when I ran out of money, a newspaper for a small town north of L.A. hired me to cover local stories about garden clubs and cutthroat knitting competitions—I'd dated the editor. I also came up with a sales training program for an upscale real estate company and tried and failed miserably to sell real estate. Along the way I peddled advertising for phonebooks and spent my nights as the old guy bartender at a beach bar and, when I snored in class, got drummed out of an intense military-like program for stockbrokers."

"Your bizarre careers are seriously funny. Maybe you should be a comedian, you know go into L.A. and audition at one of the comedy clubs. Show business has to be the only career you haven't tried." Constance crossed her arms and took a second look at the exit sign.

I admit my job list seemed otherworldly, like it wasn't really me who'd had those jobs. Constance took out a small notebook, scribbled something in it and frowned.

"For a few weeks, to get in shape, I cut lawns and trimmed hedges with a group of college guys. My first clue I didn't belong came when the crew nicknamed me gramps. Oh, and at night I stumbled into selling premium wines. In the summer I led a conditioning program at a retirement home. At least I got some rest while we all sat in chairs and did arm and leg lifts."

"Nothing you've done makes sense. Okay, no one would deny you're interesting, like some kind of a make-believe character, but you're a drifter who's way, way too far out for me." Constance stood, adjusted her gold coat and headed in the direction of the exit sign.

It didn't require a major insight to see my job history wasn't a good topic if I wanted a second date with a successful woman. Listening to that list of jobs brought me one of those electrifying reality moments. After the divorce and being abandoned in the beach cottage, I contracted commitment phobia. Relationships, jobs, even the places I lived, I didn't want anything permanent, especially nothing smacking of obligation.

I'd gotten hooked on being rootless and not knowing what I'd be doing from week to week. If I didn't have any strong connections, even a steady job, I didn't have to be against anything.

A couple of days after Constance left I started a second list, women I'd dated. My relationships mirrored my job history. I'd gone out with teachers, nurses, a college professor, a psychologist and two exotic dancers and made a badly failed attempt at attracting a magazine publisher. With no attachments and no one to criticize me, I didn't have a sense that years were going by. For the first time in a decade dad came back into my mind. He'd been a wanderer without any plan or purpose and he'd drifted through his life. I'd sworn I'd never be like him.

I'd repeated his pattern, except maybe I had a slightly different motivation; all the jobs and relationships were my way of protecting myself by not getting too involved in my own life.

I needed an immediate change and said what I was thinking out loud. "Court, you can't keep adding to your ridiculous job history. Find something you care about."

Time to get serious. Writing had been my only constant. I hadn't published anything and wasn't satisfied with what I'd written. It would be a long, tough road to become a successful writer. Still what I put on paper mattered to me and kept me sane. What if I made a U-turn and put all my energies into storytelling?

STITCHING – <u>Connecting Scenes Four and Five:</u>

It's easy to slip into wandering; that's what my illogical job history taught me. On the plus side of the ledger I'd opened up to new experiences and understood the world had more layers than I imagined. My judgments and prejudices had slipped away.

At night in secret I'd write short stories, ones about beasts or mythical creatures, and knights and adventures, like the tales I'd tell my kids before the divorce. Through all the jobs and relationships those stories stayed as the only constant in my life.

Sylvia's Scene Four

Four Divorces

It's almost impossible for me to imagine anyone can have one marriage and find real love the first time. I've had four divorces, four losses I measure my life by.

The first marriage, a teenage rebellion, I did my best to make work and stayed long enough to have my two daughters. I took away an extra share of fear and bewilderment from a divorce at such a young age. A second marriage and divorce, doomed by mutual not ready for commitment, left me angry, devastated, feeling betrayed and in shock. The sadness, grief and heartbreak hit hard. For weeks I slept almost around the clock.

My third marriage, where I thought I'd found a best friend I could be with for life, should have been different. Fate held other ideas. The unforeseen circumstances, a sliding house and a shattered ankle, worked against us like an evil genie's curse. Another divorce threw me into a despair and hopelessness and left me feeling I couldn't trust myself in relationships.

Marriage four is where I thought I'd finally been repaid for surviving my past divorces. I knew I'd found the love of my life. When my marriage bubble burst I hit rock bottom. More than the first three divorces combined, the last breakup devastated me. The combination of anger, the heartbreak, and the deep, deep grief turned into an emotional storm I didn't think I could survive.

The third and fourth marriages came with a growing realization I needed to change. Looking back at marriage three the move to the city bought challenges none of us expected. For a while Jake worked for his father. He tried and failed to start a business, attempted to sell real estate and finally went back into construction. His job meant over the next few years he came home only sporadically.

The girls left their friends in the mountains and started a new school at mid-year. We lived in a rental and with Jake and me working they were on their own after school. Two lonely, unhappy pre-teen girls made the best of the difficult situation and so did we.

I began a new career at a real estate company—Poppie had passed on to me his belief in land and home ownership. I had to put all my energies into building my own business clientele and worked seven days a week and some evenings. The pressure and pressing financial needs turned me into a workaholic and emotionally distant mother.

Somehow we survived the next several years, until I had enough business to buy a single-level tract home. We moved again.

My relationship with Jake is the price I paid for throwing everything into my career. We just wore each other out. At least Jake and I parted as friends. The burden of divorce three fell on my girls. Losing their home and security gone again devastated them.

I suffered too. The years of non-stop work combined with another emotionally trying time left me with what the doctor called "burnout". For a month I couldn't make myself work.

When I did go back to real estate with a growing company, my drive to succeed got me promoted to a management position.

That's when I met the man who became my fourth husband. I remember my mother telling me, "Sylvia, he's tall, handsome and a professional. He's the one. Make this marriage work."

For a while it felt like I had my Prince Charming and didn't need to pay attention to the practical realities of life. I sold my home and we bought a larger one for our expanded family, his two teenage boys and my two teenage girls—imagine four teenagers who don't know each other trying to get along. We tried to make it work, but coming from very different lifestyles doomed our best attempts. My oldest left to attend college, and my younger daughter moved into an apartment and started to study accounting at a business college.

Along with the growing family problems, we'd made risky real estate investments, including developing a condominium complex on a beautiful lake in Florida. We'd mortgaged our home and another property to do this "quick turn-around project." About the time we finished the project the marketplace changed and interest rates soared.

In a panic I quit my job, moved to Florida, lived in one of the condos and tried to sell them. There were no buyers. In lieu of foreclosure, we turned the complex over to the bank.

Everything fell apart. We lost the project and our investment, had to sell our home at a loss, and turned our other property over to the bank. The hard work and struggles to re-build our lives disappeared down a rabbit hole. It's no surprise the marriage didn't survive.

Divorce four, the worst of my devastating losses, left me unemployed, penniless and in such a heart broken state all I could do was cry. I felt defeated and admitted life had broken me. For the first time I gave in and surrendered.

It's my third marriage where I wished I'd tried harder. Jake and I were good friends and cared deeply about each other and our family. It saddens me I let go of the relationship without more conscious effort to save it. A few years ago Jake passed away from an unexpected heart attack. I regret I never told him how much his friendship, help, and love meant to me and my girls.

Four marriages gave me a unique perspective. For so long I believed nothing could ever break my spirit. Not true. The heartbreak of each divorce left me feeling like I'd endured ongoing torture. Angry and disillusioned, I finally broke down and retreated into a shell.

STITCHING – <u>Connecting Scenes Four and Five:</u>

I didn't need another divorce to realize I'd repeated a pattern. Anger and frustration had taken over my life. I desperately needed professional help. I'd go on my own quest to find a way to break my destructive pattern and another way to live life.

Tell * Journal * Write

Scene Four

Empathy is part of coaching. We understand you'll do your best to describe what it feels like to have no direction or purpose, and you'll tell, journal or write about how time in the wilderness gave you the opportunity to pick a new direction for your life. This scene needs to show solitary introspection, and reflection, a sense of drifting and emotionally apart from the world. Your challenge is to describe what it feels like to be in a private limbo and have to struggle to discover a path back to the world.

Your core sentence establishes a confused and bewildered feeling that produces both fear and tension that you'll be trapped in a wanderer's bland life

Court's **core sentence** moves in a different direction, "On a coffee date I finally accepted having eleven jobs in four years isn't a good discussion topic for a lasting relationship." He's counted up the number of jobs he's had and maybe for the first time begins to understand his list of strange jobs reveals the nonsensical nature of wandering and what it means to be rootless.

Sylvia's **core paragraph** features four divorces as a symbol of wandering and illustrates her bewilderment. "It's almost impossible for me to imagine anyone can have one marriage and find real love the first time. I've had four divorces, four losses I measure my life by."

Don't pull punches in your scene and don't try to look good. Wandering won't present you in the best light. Set up a contrast between rootless drifting and the committed zeal of a quest.

Backstory is important in wandering. A connection between the past and the future is often the best way to see the motivation behind wandering. Court writes how he realizes he's repeating his father's pattern. "For the first time in a decade dad came back into my mind. He'd been a wanderer without any plan or purpose and he'd drifted through his life. I'd sworn I'd never be like him and I'd repeated his pattern ……..." Sylvia senses even her career choice is partly motivated by her ongoing need to please her grandfather. "I began a new career at a real estate company—Poppie had passed on his belief in land and home ownership."

Another way to use **backstory** is to tell, journal or write what you daydreamed about in childhood. Go back in time to when you were four to ten years old and see your youth through those memories. What did you love to do and think about? What things did you dream about doing you now think are silly or not possible? Did you have special heroes or people you wanted to grow up to be like? Did you like to draw, paint or do projects with your hands? Your answers to those questions could access long repressed memories containing clues to beginning a quest you've secretly wanted to undertake.

Turning point moments, where wandering ends and a quest begins are a major shift in your perspective as you journey through the cycle. A change of direction in your story, a turning point, needs to be present in every scene. It's there to signal a change in viewpoint and reflect the growth necessary to move through the journey.

The turning point you craft most carefully is where you move out of wandering to engage the quest. This new focus is the true cycle change point. The past and future are finally at a level place and the journey begins the upward climb. There is a concurrence of old limitations and new possibilities in your journey, and foresight takes over from back sight. You have a chance to begin again.

Each of your scenes should have its own turning point, a different moment of clarity. Words or phrases you might use with scene turning points are crossroad, flashpoint, moment of truth, watershed moment, crux, reality check and turn of the tide. Court's confrontation with his father, his divorce, and being abandoned in the beach house were pivotal moments in his Cycle Journey. Sylvia leaving her grandparents, her sliding house and her broken leg became defining moments for her.

Turning points offer endless descriptive options. You could:

- Reach the mountain top.
- Have your eyes opened.

- Know the planets aligned.
- Feel like a new day is starting.
- Have a heads up feeling.
- Get a go ahead signal.
- Arrive at the place where down meets up.

The turning point needs to be recognizable. Court's is, "Listening to all those jobs brought me one of those electrifying reality moments. After the divorce and being abandoned in the beach cottage, I contracted commitment phobia." Sylvia expresses her turning point moment in her stitching when she writes, "I didn't need another divorce to realize I'd repeated a similar pattern and anger and frustration had taken over my life. I desperately needed professional help. I'd go on my own quest to find a way to break my destructive pattern and another way to live life."

In wandering words provide atmosphere and mood. Here are wandering words. Put some of them into your scene and you'll find it almost writes itself.

Disoriented	Rootless	In A Void
Disconnected	Roving	Confusion
Blind Stumbling	Purposelessness	Meandering
An Escape	Peter Pan-Like	Perpetual
Rambling	Outlier	Boredom
Lost	Aimless	A Breakaway
Drifting	In Never Land	Gone Astray
Nomadic	Recycling	

In the last paragraph tell about the **deepened insights and expanded awareness** you've realized that point to the direction you'll take to move out of wandering.

FIVE

The Red Stage, Quest

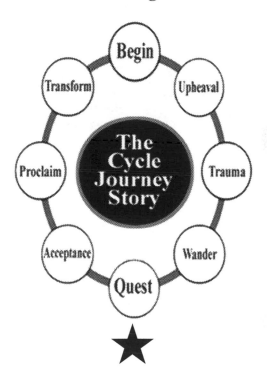

The Energy and Action Commitment
"If you can see your path laid out in front of you step by
step, you know it's not your path. Your own path you make
with every step you take. That's why it's your path."
~Joseph Campbell, Author, Philosopher and Teacher

An Introduction To Stage Five

You've been emboldened, filled with courage and purpose, by engaging a quest. The journey has reached mid-point. You know successful quests aren't random undertakings and are committed to begin a planned search for an authentic destiny.

More than the other stages there are an abundance of cultural quest examples—King Arthur, *Lord of the Rings* and *Don Quixote*. The quest's Deeper Insight is the beginning Individuation or seeing yourself as unique. Humpty Dumpty is off on his quest and we are looking for ways to define ourselves and exploring possible quests of our own.

Stage Five's Tell * Journal * Write coaching section challenges you to describe your feelings and emotions attached to this adventure.

The Essentials

It may be a leap of faith to say there's always been a place in the world, a fore-ordained destiny waiting for you. Transforming, the ability to be a new you suggests fate isn't inevitable and even a destiny isn't a natural occurrence. It has to be claimed. As it was for the Grail knights, it is the claiming process which proves you worthy of what awaits at the end of the adventure.

A quest, the cycle's red stage, is an energy-filled undertaking where a quester metaphorically or realistically leaves home for the unknown. This separation allows space for a newfound calling to take shape and an authentic Self to appear out of a new destiny.

A quest is a committed personal journey, a thrilling adventure and an essential step in claiming a new life path. The red stage symbolizes summoning the strength and power accompanying the quester's pledge to commit to a triumphant quest. That promise becomes a bright light capable of burning away the Dark Night.

This turning point in the cycle is where the focus shifts from absorbing the upheaval's blow to moving toward a true transformation.

There is risk and peril, even the possibility of significant loss attached to the tests the quester is required to pass to be deemed worthy of claiming whatever waits at the end of the journey.

Often, during the quest the true goal becomes clearer, evolves, or changes. Part of what fills a quest with momentous consequence and turns it into the center point in a Cycle Journey is that its results and successes are not predetermined.

Quests Have Eight Components:
One: Commit to undertake a meaningful quest. Commitment to a quest must be made with an all in attitude. Allow yourself to do something not easy, but necessary so you can be in alignment with your true Self. This is a pledge where there is a requirement for strength of mind and spirit and a total focus of will.

Sir Gallant's quest begins: Imagine a true knight's quest where the hero, the handsome and courageous Sir Gallant the Brave, is called to King Reginald's throne room. The king tells him the dastardly Duke Blackmore has kidnapped his daughter, the beautiful Princess Eleanor. A look of resolute determination flashes across Gallant's face. He holds his shield in front of him and raises his sword.

Two: Listen to inner whisperings about your choices before you announce the quest. Let creativity, imagination and intuition play their role. Quest selection can be rooted in childhood experiences, a dream job, a forgotten idea or invention. There will be quests that seem more glamorous and more profitable, but there should be only one pursuit that stirs you at a deep enough level to lead to a personal transformation.

Sir Gallant hears the call: The brave knight pushes back his blond hair, closes his eyes and looks deep into his heart. With absolute conviction he swears an oath loud enough for everyone at court to hear. "This is it, my one true quest and I swear by the knight's Code of Chivalry, even if it costs me my life, I'll rescue the princess."

Three: Have a quest plan. Planning should include a design for executing the quest. It can be done on a computer or in a quest journal where you jot down ideas and steps you'll take to complete a quest. Make the plan personal by writing about where you think the pursuit will be hard and where you believe you might have to face your own fears.

Sir Gallant plans: Our hero-knight develops his quest plan by visiting a monastery to check parchment maps that tell how to avoid dragons. He also reads tales the monk scribes have written about the duke and the dangers of his castle. He tells the king and his fellow knights his feelings about how this quest will test his bravery.

Four: Prepare for the quest. Whether it's a different computer, books to increase knowledge about the quest landscape, new tools or necessary repairs, a quester needs meticulous preparation. There are equal amounts of fear and exhilaration that arise out of a dawning realization you're a committed and there's no going back.

Gallant prepares for his adventure: Once he has his plan of attack in mind, he polishes his armor, sharpens his sword, sands the rust off his lance and, in front of the worried king practices his knightly fighting skills. Only when he is sure his preparation is complete does Gallant announce, "I am ready to save the fair princess."

Five: Engage a quest. Whether engaging is talking to people who work for the company you're interviewing or mortgaging a home to start a new company, there's an understanding this is a full-blown adventure undertaken without reservations. You are committed to do whatever is necessary to make the pursuit real.

Sir Gallant sets his adventure in motion: Our fearless knight, with an imaginary picture of fair Eleanor fixed in his mind and his well-polished armor gleaming in the sun, kicks the quest into gear by talking to other knights who have visited Blackmore's castle. He goes so far as to ride to another castle to learn from a fellow knight about the Duke's tactics and his strategy with the sword and lance.

Six: Move toward the core of the quest. In some fashion you must leave the comfort of your normal world. If you're starting a company, the core of the quest might be renting office space and if you're going to explore Africa, making airline reservations could launch your quest.

Sir Gallant departs the castle: Prepared in every conceivable way, the brave knight waves his gloved hand in the air, salutes the king, saddles up and, to the cheers of the castle inhabitants shouts out, "Let my adventure begin. Soon the evil duke will know what it is like to meet a knight who has the right on his side." He rides through the gates and, without ever looking back, heads for the evil duke's fortress.

Seven: Overcome obstacles in the way of completion. Surmounting difficulties and achieving fulfillment brings a feeling of real growth and the first signs of the coming transformation are evident. Whether you have overcome a critic or successfully dealt with a difficult customer, old limitations no longer hold you back.

Sir Gallant vanquishes the enemy: The brave warrior has lived up to the knight's code of chivalry by cutting down scores of the enemy. He stands in the middle of Blackmore's body-filled castle courtyard, his foot on the dead duke's chest. Cuts cover his face and arms and he feels every bit the true hero.

Eight: Fulfill the quest then learn from its results. The quest should to some degree alter the course of your life. A new job makes every day stimulating, a fresh painting style breaks old boundaries, or moving to a new city makes each moment exciting. Your world view has enlarged. There is a new flow of deep insights and a feeling your awareness has dramatically expanded.

Sir Gallant is victorious: The adoring Lady Eleanor is at Gallant's side. His few living enemies have realized his just cause led to their defeat. He heads back to the castle, once again confirming being a knight isn't about titles or riches. It's a spiritual calling requiring the courage to pursue a prize of great value. With the king and the other knights watching in admiration, Gallant gets down on one knee and tells Lady Eleanor, "The true love I feel for you has given my life new meaning and purpose."

Heroic questers like Sir Gallant take impossible chances as they venture into a world of unexpected dangers and challenges. Some survive and some don't. Some complete their quest while other equally brave questers end the pursuit knowing only failure.

The quest's eight steps take the Cycle Journey out of darkness and into the light. Each step requires increasing involvement and commitment from the quester. Discovered at the end of the exploit is a new destiny that needs to be accepted and proclaimed to the world.

The quest opens up a world of new possibilities. It can be seen as the first definitive move toward individuation and fulfilling an innate urge toward wholeness and balance. More than that there is a call to serve a higher purpose, which must be the motivation of every quester. In contrast, if the quest does not serve a higher purpose, individuation is blocked, and the conscious and unconscious are unable to unite.

An authentic quest, like King Arthur's knights and their search for the fabled Holy Grail, is a pursuit undertaken to find or obtain a prize so great it will advance the quester mentally and spiritually. Arthur's knights undertook multiple quests as they searched for the prized Holy Grail, the symbol of spiritual wholeness. In true quest fashion, some, like Percival and Sir Galahad, succeeded while other heroes like Sir Lancelot, failed to measure up to the challenges and pass the tests required to prove them worthy to claim the prize.

In contrast, another famous quest tale, *Don Quixote*, is a parody of the knight's quest. His mock pursuit, really aimless wandering, makes him a fool and yet his gallantry for gallantry's sake turned him into a hero for the ages. He says, "Bear in mind, Sancho, that one man is no more than another, unless he does more than another." That quote shows he has grasped at its core a quest strives to exceed limitations.

Lord of the Rings is an unrivaled quest epic where the least likely quester becomes the hero of the adventure. Frodo Baggin's steadfast quest to destroy the One Ring turns him into one of literature's greatest characters. In *The Two Towers* he states, "I am commanded to go to the land of Mordor, and therefore I shall go,' said Frodo. 'If there is only one way then I must take it. What comes after must come." He expresses the essence of a quest.

Not all quests are pure or lead to a true destiny. A dark quest with a baser intent, such as Mordred, Arthur's illegitimate son and his treachery in trying to steal Arthur's throne, is an unprincipled search for power or wealth and is a pursuit where the ends justify the means. The dark quest appeals to baser motives like greed, lust, dominance, and status and follows a shadowy, soul-destroying road.

Quest messages create an Active Imagination inspiration for an adventure by appearing in different creative and imaginative forms, dreams, visions, intuition, symbols, hunches, or from meditation, books, movies, music or nature. Each message type leads the quester closer to becoming who he or she was meant to be, living the life they deserve, and discovering an authentic destiny.

The mythological quest, in contrast to the knight's quest, has most often been called the Hero's Journey. It's a dramatic structure found in countless stories, books and movies. The Cycle Journey quest takes the same courage and tenacity as the Hero's Journey or knight's quest. The intense inner journey searches for the identical authentic destiny the hero or the knight seeks.

Doctor Carol Pearson describes a quest in her introduction to *Awakening the Heroes Within*. "For the Hero's Journey is first about taking a journey to find the treasure of your true self and then returning home to give your gift to help transform the kingdom—and in the process your own life. The quest itself is replete with danger and pitfalls, but it offers great rewards: the capacity to be successful in the world, knowledge of the mysteries of the human soul, the opportunity to find and express your unique gifts in the world, and to live in loving community with other people...Heroism is also not just about finding a new truth, but about having the courage to act on the vision."

After fulfilling the quest, there are important questions the quester must ask:

- Has the quest, as if it has always been waiting for the quester to enact it, seemed inevitable?
- Is there a sense of destiny attached to this quest?

If your instincts say this is your quest and there's a feeling of inevitability about what you've undertaken, you're on the right path. If your answers make you uncomfortable or ill at ease, you need to refine your pursuit or pursue another quest.

Stage 5 Deeper Insight

Individuation

"I will try to explain the term 'individuation' as simply as possible. By it I mean the psychological process that makes of a human being an 'individual' – a unique, indivisible unit of 'whole man.'" ~ C. G. Jung

The first step in selecting a quest is to see yourself as an individual with a unique destiny. Individuation is the gradual integration and merger of the Self through resolving successive layers of inner conflict. It develops the whole and balanced personality which forms a stable individual. It's the heartbeat of change. People who move through the cycle stages toward transformation reflect their true Self by becoming more harmonious, mature, and responsible. They promote freedom and make decisions based on a good understanding of human nature.

Individuation makes you aware of your internal makeup and defines a true Self. It uses inner wisdom to answer the quest's central question "who am I." You are able to embrace your uniqueness. Individuation achieves the wholeness and balance at the core of every transformation.

Grow yourself through self-knowledge and it's likely your consciousness won't be held captive by petty, personal interests. This expanded view directed by the Self moves past worrisome fears, trivial desires, and self-serving ambitions. Instead an outlook centered on developing a relationship with the larger world is embraced.

In the quest individuation attempts to unite the conscious and the unconscious. The word comes from the Latin *individuus* meaning undivided or individual. Jung believed individuation is the process of differentiation—the development of the personality where a person becomes separate and whole.

Individuation taps into the inner world. Jung wasn't the first to propose the concept of individuation. For more than a thousand years Taoists and Buddhists promoted its importance. The benefits of individuation are:

- You stay in harmony and don't act against your nature.
- You conform to your true Self.
- You live in relationship with the life your soul intends for you.
- You are liberated from parents and form your individuality.

Especially in the quest, acceptance, and proclaiming the pace of individuation increases. By the eighth stage, transformation, there is a new level of uniting of the conscious and unconscious.

The Stories For Stage Five

<u>Humpty's Scene Five:</u>

Committed

Years of caution have done no good. He's ended up with the cracks and pieces of missing shell he's lived his entire life trying to avoid. What surprises him is a new sense of liberation.

<u>Court's Scene Five:</u>

My Adventure

I had a sense of purpose, not a feeling I had to protect myself.

<u>Sylvia's Scene Five:</u>

Moving On

The best way to describe what's happened to me is it feels like I've put myself in a deep hole and the time has come to stop digging.

<u>Your Cycle Journey Story:</u>

Scene Five - The Quest

Humpty's Story Continues:
Chapter Five: Committed

Filled with enthusiasm, the next day Humpty is up at the first crack of dawn and in the carton's kitchen humming and drinking a cup of lima bean coffee as he reads what he wrote yesterday. It comes to him he's lived most of his life feeling like he walked on egg shells. Over the years he'd done everything possible to follow his father's advice. The extremes he went to now seem ridiculous. To guard his breakable shell he slept on double mattresses, put pads around the bed and rubbed a nightly coat of wax into his shell.

Years of caution have done no good. He's ended up with the cracks and pieces of missing shell he's lived his entire life trying to avoid. What surprises him is a new sense of liberation.

For the first time Humpty counts the other pluses in his life. His egg white, his albumen, is still healthy and the thicker ropes of egg white, the chalazae which hold his yoke feel stronger than ever. What's more he's not so concerned with the opinions of others and senses his core, his yoke, is denser than it's been in years. The work he put into writing about his great fall added a new clarity to his life.

Humpty grabs the countertop with both hands. As the sun rises and its golden rays fill the kitchen, he has an overpowering inspiration. He's recalled a dream about summer camp and how, in spite of his damaged shell, he imagined himself as a leader to the young eggs.

Right then and there he makes a life-changing commitment. He'll follow that dream and do what it takes to work with the kingdom's egglets. He can tell them they can be every bit as good as a Faberge egg and there's much more to life than being obsessed with shell appearance.

This quest, to be a counselor to young eggs will be a new direction for his life. He'll have to return to college to study egg physiology and early egg education. He may even enroll at Ovum Medical School. It'll take years of study to learn how embryos grow and master the techniques for strengthening the character of the egglets he'll be expected to guide to maturity. His expertise will be using his great fall to explain sitting on a wall above it all won't help the youngsters reach their full potential.

This new destiny is a stunning revelation. Still the change of career seems right, like something waiting in the shadows for years. He wonders why he didn't see this path before. There's a blossoming sense of purpose he's never known. Ideas for creative ways to encourage the young eggs are flowing so fast he feels overwhelmed.

Humpty's new direction for his life isn't greeted with universal acclaim. Before she leaves to spend the weekend with her mother-in-law, his wife's tears drip down his shell as she tells him, "My dear, can't you see ever since the fall you've acted like a different egg? If you really cared about me and the egglets, you'd go to the hatchery and plead with the big boss to give you your job back."

Two hours after his wife's departure Humpty's father, so upset his brown shell has turned bright red, barges into the carton. He waves his fist inches from his son's shell. "Your dear poor wife came to our carton in tears. She told your mother and me about your educational fantasy. My boy, your brain is scrambled. We've been patient with you, but enough is enough. This change of careers pipedream is going to ruin your family. Your mother and your wife are back at the carton so upset they are ready to jump into a frying pan." Humpty's father storms out the door.

Not knowing what else to do, Humpty walks out to the mailbox. Inside there's an envelope with a red rejected stamp. Ovum Medical College has sent him a form letter telling Humpty he's far too old to start their rigorous curriculum.

His wife, father, mother, and the medical school won't stop him. Humpty refuses to back away from his vision of the future. He knows working with young eggs is his true calling and he no longer needs all the king's horses and all the king's men or advice from family, friends and coworkers. He has himself, the one and only Humpty Dumpty. He imagines he's one of the old egg knights charging out of the castle filled with the commitment and courage necessary for a life-changing adventure.

Court's Scene Five

My Adventure

I'd found a home, but had no career or consuming passion. I needed a purpose, something I wanted to do more than anything else. After all I'd been through, the divorce, the failed relationships and the crazy list of jobs, none of it would be worth much if I couldn't find that one elusive piece of fate that held my authentic destiny.

One day it came to me like an inner whispering that I'd spent too much time protecting myself from dad's dark prophecy. To focus on something I was for instead of against, I signed up for my first writer's conference, a six day event more than two-hundred writers would attend. There'd be workshops and late-night sessions where writers could read their stories and get a critique from instructors.

I trained for the conference by reading and rereading every book and article I had on writing and spent days picking out the sessions I'd attend. For once I had a sense of purpose, not a feeling I had to protect myself.

The night before the conference I had a dream about my writing insecurities. On a stage in front of hundreds of people I started my story. Before I finished a sentence someone laughed. There were giggles then chuckles. Within seconds everyone in the audience hooted and started rolling in the aisles.

The next morning to get the nightmare out of my head and prove my intention to get everything possible out of the conference, I got to the beachside hotel early enough to be one of the first people in line when they opened the doors to the ballroom. Every person carried their laptop or an armload of over-stuffed notebooks. They looked as lost as I felt. Until now I'd seen writing as a lonely profession.

To try and make sure I at least looked the part and everyone could see at first glance I had serious writer aspirations, I'd gone a little over the top and researched writer images on the computer. My khaki sport coat, jeans, and a denim shirt were the same outfit I'd seen on a famous writer signing autographs for his new bestseller.

I set my triple latte on the table, signed in, got a light blue round badge with my name in extra-large red letters and young adult fantasy writer below it then headed for my first seminar on how to write fantasy and science fiction.

It wasn't hard to imagine dad beside me laughing as he gloated, "Kid, this isn't any different from the band. You don't have the talent and you'll quit. You failed then and you'll fail again."

A few minutes later ten of us sat around a table. The bearded instructor stood and asked our names. I felt a cold chill. This was it and my battle to prove I could be a real writer had been engaged.

The heavy-set instructor introduced himself as Raymond Levias. He put his hands on the table. "Writers and pretend writers, I'm the author of ten fantasy novels and before we start reading I want to give you a reality check on what it takes to get published."

Raymond scratched his beard and smiled. "I don't care if you are the next Hemingway or Virginia Wolfe, on your first fifty quires to agents consider yourself lucky to get more than two or three responses and those will be polite form letter turndowns."

Levias flashed a nasty grin. "I'm just getting warmed up. It gets worse, much worse. Of course, you might be one of the chosen few who is asked to send in a manuscript. Don't get your hopes up. You're not anywhere close to the bestseller table. Expect what you've written to sit on the agents desk for two or three months while he or she is busy attending writer's conferences like this."

Everyone had their eyes on the tabletop. There were nervous coughs. Raymond's smile seemed even more gloating. "Now for the hard part, the critics. Everyone you know, parents, relatives, friends, strangers, and anyone you let read your story is going to pick at your work. Even worse most of what you hear won't be worth warm spit, but the critics will insist you follow their advice to the letter."

Raymond walked around the table like a drill sergeant who couldn't believe his naive rookie charges. "Writing is a job, a damn tough job where your story won't start to get good until you've put it through what will seem like countless revisions. By the time you finish a book, if you've done the work you'll be so sick of your characters the sound of their names will make you physically ill—and that is the easy part." His voice growled. "Critics will have picked at every line, every word choice and every comma until you don't have a shred of self-esteem left."

"The way you're talking we should give up and go home." The young girl kept her eyes on the ceiling. I could see tears on her cheeks.

I kept quiet, but the part about critics hit home. I don't do well with detractors and faultfinders. Deep down I know that's one of the reasons I'd held back on showing anyone what I'd written.

"My job is to introduce you to the real world of writers." Levias' voice got softer. "Listen carefully boys and girls, everyone falls in love with the romance of writing not the work. Writing is lonely and miserably hard and the chances of success aren't great. My first lesson is if you don't absolutely love writing and aren't willing to sacrifice practically anything to keep writing, don't waste everyone's time, go home now."

Maybe Levias pushed too hard. Two people, the younger girl who'd asked the last question and was now wiping a flow of tears from her eyes and a middle aged guy got up and left.

Raymond, like he couldn't help himself, flashed a victorious grin. "Good, now I can invest my time in serious writers. Over the next few days I'll give you practical tips on what it takes to get published. Each day you'll have fifteen minutes to read. Everyone comments on what they've heard. My inputs will be last and since I assume you all want to get published, they'll be brutally honest."

We drew numbers out of a hat. I'd go fourth—this would be the first time I'd read before fellow writers—and Raymond Levias. The first story about a flyer in World War II who flew into a cloud and came out in a land ruled by wizards had tons of information on wizard costumes and not much plot or suspense. Everyone tried to be nice. I could tell no one loved the tale.

Raymond didn't pull punches. "It's boring. If I was a wizard I'd find a more exciting job. Anyway your magical world doesn't have enough magic." The guy's frown dropped so low I thought his self-confidence had fallen into his lap.

I was so jittery I felt I'd had ten cups of coffee. The second would-be writer read a story about a college girl with a mean fraternity boyfriend who happened to be a shape-shifted troll. This story went over a little better.

Raymond didn't try to be encouraging. "The only thing obvious in your story is you haven't really thought about what it means to be a troll. I don't care if it's a monster or not, the troll needs a personality and a reason why it's managed to stay hidden on a college campus." I felt like one of those toys at a carnival barker's booth waiting to get baseballs thrown at it.

The third story had a 1920's vampire bootlegger recall his life, scrapes with the law and how he mixed different types of blood in his popular moonshine. This one sounded pretty good. I couldn't figure out why it hadn't already been published.

"Why did a vampire become a bootlegger—what's his backstory? How does he know what kind of blood to mix in his moonshine? Does he have an ancient family formula? Isn't he afraid the local sheriff might drive a stake through him? Do the young coeds think he's sexy? You have too many unanswered questions. Regardless of how fantastic they are, a monster or fantasy story has to have characters the reader imagines could exist." The way Raymond cut into a story he should have been a surgeon.

My turn came. I took a large gulp of latte and plunged forward. "My story is about a genius leprechaun, Finn Doyle, who refused to wear green."

Everyone nodded. Raymond smiled. My voice quivered as I pressed on. "Finn Doyle's tale begins with the leprechaun leaders, the Himselfs, making a special trek across the Leprechaun Underground to convince Doyle of the ages-old wisdom of wearing green."

More laughs. Raymond stayed quiet. I used different voices for the characters and an Irish brogue, doing everything possible to make the story come alive.

My first real audience seemed to like Finn Doyle. There were suggestions on how I could build the suspense and tension, most of which I agreed with.

Raymond stayed quiet. The group ended and people came up and told me they couldn't wait to hear more of Finn's adventures.

Raymond dismissed the class. Before I could leave he pulled me to the side. "Not bad, fun concept, but Finn Doyle needs to show more of his genius, maybe like the Himselfs are jealous of him. What about if he goes into the human world and makes a fortune. You need to do some deep thinking about what you're trying to accomplish with this story. One piece of advice, the screwy writer costume you're trying to impress everybody with tells me you may not have the depth of character to pull off a first-class story." Raymond Levias shook his head and walked out of the room.

Okay, it would take more than a costume to be a good writer. Levias' class marked the defining moment, a point where I committed to a quest to be a writer. I had a spooky feeling I'd been put on earth to come up with fantastic new myths and make ancient history come to life. By the way I threw the writer costume in the trash.

After Levias' class Dad and his you're not good enough putdowns faded into the background. I had a new sense of how much I had to learn, creating characters readers care about, the importance of the opening chapter, realistic dialogue, clever plots, knowing how to construct scenes, adding compelling imagery and so much more. I knew I'd get tons more critical feedback. There are days I've doubted myself. Every once in a while I've heard a faint hissing whisper that sounds like dad.

STITCHING – Connecting Scenes Five and Six:

I'd committed to my adventure and put myself out on a limb. My challenge is to learn to write at a deeper level, then go deeper. It didn't take long to find out how hard it is to become a published writer. Short stories, novels, even a half-hearted attempt at a Gothic romance, after a few years I had two more boxes full of fiction, most of which no one but me had seen.

Sylvia's Scene Five

Moving On

I'd written about how I felt after four divorces. "I'm broken into pieces. I can't tough my way through the heartbreak of my fourth divorce. What's happened to me is it feels like I've put myself in a deep hole and the time has come to stop digging."

The half of a friend's garage, turned into a tiny studio, had become my new home. After weeks of crying, sleeping, staring at the wall and telling my friend about my heartbreak, everything seemed fuzzy and disoriented. One night I found myself curled up in a fetal position on the floor. Awful moaning and wailing filled the small room. It took a few seconds to realize I'd made those scary noises. That's when I knew I needed help.

My new therapist, Beth, a tiny woman who dressed in bright tie-dyed shirts, had a way of radiating confidence. At our first meeting I started sobbing and unloaded my fears. "I've totally messed up my life. I can't function, I'm dying inside and I don't know what to do."

She took charge. "I can help. Here's what we'll do." Her soft, calm voice offered hope. I saw her twice a week. Our sessions provided the stability and something to hold onto while I struggled to find a job.

Those weekly individual and group sessions continued for three years, until she left for an extended retreat. During our time together I vowed not to get involved in a new relationship. The time alone allowed me to regain my balance, begin to heal and start to build a new life. I borrowed some money and bought a condo with my daughter. After her marriage, I lived alone and with a collection of housemates, joined a weekly women's support group and began to take an interest in life. My emotions swung up and down. One day I'd feel empowered. The next I'd be mired in loneliness and hopelessness.

I took classes in meditation, massage, healing hands of light, Reiki energy work, an experiential class in drumming and other forms of anger release and the *Course of Miracles*, read a six-foot-high stack of self-help, metaphysical and spiritual books and started to get insights into how I could get more out of my life.

Years later Beth moved back to town. In a year of intensive therapy she talked about becoming a whole person by accepting my various parts, what she called acts. We spent months getting me to see some of those parts or acts like the sad child, the angry teenager, the vulnerable victim, and the tough business woman and how they played a role in my repeating relationships. I began to have an awareness of myself at a deeper level. Journal writing about my traumatic times helped me take in the new knowledge.

Near the end of the year I walked up to her colonial house ready for one of our regular sessions. Beth wore a formal white blouse when she met me at the door, something she had never done before. In a strange formal tone she announced she'd prepared a simple vegetarian meal. Her two long-haired cats roamed around the dining room while she, her contractor husband and I ate. Beth directed the conversation toward all the things we'd done, especially how significant our chair work had been.

At the start of a session I'd sit in the one Beth called the Persona chair. The other, she christened the Self chair. In the Persona Chair I'd speak easily and carry on a regular conversation. In the Self Chair, where I talked from my inner Self, I sounded like a different person. I'd grip the arms and often become asthmatic. Sometimes I'd cry or go speechless or only speak in a raspy whisper. Over time in the Self chair I gained new confidence and my voice became stronger and clearer. Tentatively at first, I talked about the heartbreak from leaving the ranch, the failed marriages and my belief I was unlovable and unworthy of a lasting relationship.

I started to understand how distorted my Self-image had become. I am lovable but needed to be more discerning, make better choices and forgive myself and others for what happened in the past. Forgiving didn't mean I condoned what others did, but I could bring those actions into the light and let go of blaming myself and others. I could finally see the disruptive beliefs and issues I'd carried with me into each relationship.

I developed a view of how I presented myself to others and the way I acted and re-acted when emotionally triggered. During one session I told Beth my acts should be made into a feature film, and picked Meryl Streep to star as me.

At the end of the dinner, as her husband cleared the table, Beth took my hand. "Sylvia, you've learned you are not your acts. There is a loveable deeper part of you. Nothing is wrong with you and you've made peace with yourself and others. You've discovered you have choices how you react under pressure, in stress, or when someone confronts you."

Where was all this going?

Beth's voice got soft and she spoke in a slow, deliberate way. "You don't have to stay stuck in past feelings and blaming yourself and others. If you choose, if you make it a clear intention, you can stop re-acting, feel the triggered feelings, but not act on them. When you let yourself embrace and fully feel the feelings they'll go away. When you allow yourself to trust your inner wisdom you'll be free from the old recurring pattern."

At the end of the meal we stood. Her husband left. Beth looked into my eyes, cleared her throat and took both of my hands. "Sylvia I've appreciated your dedication to your healing and I've enjoyed working with you. The rest of the journey is for you to take on your own. This is the end of our time together, you have to go."

I reeled back.

"You have to go." She gave a brief smile, hugged me and opened the door.

The "you have to go" words played over and over. In a split second everything changed. For surprise it equaled my grandparents telling me I had to live with strangers. Beth walked me out on the front porch. I stumbled down the stairs and grabbed onto the hedges as I zigzagged down the sidewalk. I got to my car and started to open the door when the words she said just before telling me I had to go came into my head. "When you let yourself embrace and fully feel the feelings they'll go away. When you allow yourself to trust your inner wisdom you'll be free from the old recurring pattern." Could it be so simple, feel the feelings and trust my inner wisdom?

Later I received a beautiful card from Beth. Inside she'd written, "You have fulfilled more than I would have ever expected in our experience of Self-convergence.... I have always had appreciation for you as a sincere Self-seeker and respect your strong will and Self-devotion. With this in mind and with school now out, I want to give you this gold star as a well-earned symbol of this Self-achievement." Beth had drawn a heart and put a gold star in the center.

Beth purposely recreated a new version of the same scene I experienced at ten years old. The dinner became a teaching moment, a time when I learned to look deeper at events which seemed to have bleak interpretations and realized the value they added to my life.

I learned I could handle the feelings of being rejected and betrayed. Rather than blaming others I could use the new knowledge to bring resolution to my old wounds. Beth's strategy worked. The time had come to let go of the old feelings and beliefs that kept me re-cycling relationships. I had the freedom to move on.

STITCHING - <u>For Scenes Five and Six:</u>

I'd always wanted to finish my education and an opportunity came to me in an unexpected but timely way. I took a class in advanced Reiki and my teacher mentioned she'd started a program at a distance learning university. My intuition kicked in and I felt my excitement grow.

Tell * Journal * Write

Scene Five

Our role in helping develop your quest scene is as a guide.

Look at scene five from the vantage point of a knight on an adventure he hopes will bring deep personal fulfillment. Your scene, your adventure, needs to contain the explosion of the energy needed for questing and at the same time show a vow to seek a new destiny.

Your quest scene should be more than a meandering diary. Fill it with commitment and excitement. What better place for Court's writing quest than a writing conference? Quest tone reflects the kind of deeper insight and expanded awareness Sylvia gained from her inner work with her therapist, Beth.

The quest is a dynamic scene filled with action. It needs to paint strong **metaphors, similes, and analogies**.

Metaphors compare something to something else. He's a slithering snake or a preying wolf are metaphors based on an implied resemblance or similarity without using like or as. A metaphor is applied to an object or concept it does not literally represent, suggesting an indirect comparison. Humpty's story is full of metaphors. There's a sunny side up life, a hardboiled dad, and a fearsome Frankenstein egg.

A **simile** takes the edge off a metaphor by comparing two things using like or as. It creates distance and makes the comparison similar, not absolutely the same. There's feeling like a homeless nomad, and an attitude like an out-of-control Napoleon.

An **analogy** is also a comparison. It reveals the unknown in terms of the known, and the unfamiliar by holding it up against the familiar. In a literal sense an analogy, the egg kingdom and all its different parts, is a spider web of metaphors and similes. The analogy does not, in the way the metaphor does, claim a total connection. It stresses a likeness by linking the major similarities of two unlike things—the egg kingdom and human kingdom.

The three forms of imagery comparison move uninteresting statements to fascinating themes and create special meanings out of ordinary experience. These comparisons lend tone and mood to your quest scene. They can be strange, inspiring, gloomy, comical, and nasty as long as they get down to the essence of what you want to say. Be economical with metaphors, similes and analogies. Extended too far they're ruined. Look for surprising comparisons.

The scene will have a **turning point** moment that shows you're ready to accept a new destiny. In Court's scene he describes his turning point this way, "Levias' class marked the defining moment, a change point for me committing to a deeper quest. For the first time I could remember, I had no sense dad was around, and the feeling I needed to protect myself wasn't there either."

Use the **eight quest parts** as your scene structure.

- Describe how you listened to inner whisperings and announced the quest to others.
- Put in a quest plan and tell how you'll prepare for the quest.
- Tell when and where you'll engage your quest and be specific about how you'll know you're at the core of the quest.
- Add to the scene what it will take to fulfill your quest and why you think this will be a change point in your life.
- Describe ways your quest has changed you. Are you more confident?
- Do you feel your life has a higher purpose?
- Do you have a new job or new friends?

The Humpty Dumpty Principle, even though we've never left home, has been our quest. Our commitment has been tested and we can clearly see the eight parts of a quest in the way we developed this book. We've learned so much the old us is no longer recognizable. Your quest scene should show the same sense of being revitalized.

Words you can use to structure your quest scene are:

Mission	A Worthy Undertaking
Hunt	A Venture
A Pursuit for Fulfillment	A Search
A Personal Journey	An Exploit into the Unknown
An Adventure	A Difficult Effort
A Seeker	Seeking Great Value

Enlarge the scope of the quest by adding extra impact to the scene with a **personal poem, a mention of music that played when you were questing, drawing or taking a photo of the setting or describing a dream.**

Poetry is lyrical, like an ancient chant reaching into the soul. You don't have to be an accomplished poet to put your feelings on paper. A poem expresses quest emotions and feelings in a stark, graphic way which would normally take paragraphs or pages. Poetry invites the mind to come up with strong imagery and key symbols. Both Court and Sylvia use poems in their beginning scene.

Drawings and photos, especially black and white pictures are images your inner world craves. A sketch of your childhood house or attaching family photos adds a visual dimension which stimulates your unconscious. In the beginning scene Sylvia took the sub-title, *I grew up on the River Ranch seeing myself as a wild child*, from a childhood photo.

Dreams can be additions that add dimension to your scenes. A non-analyzed dream description adds depth and brings your unconscious directly into your writing. Court's nightmare in his quest scene shows how much fear he has about reading before an audience.

Music like poetry touches our emotions. Favorite songs, tunes which were playing at critical times and special singers who reach our feelings and stay in the unconscious. Describing a melody or adding lyrics increases the dramatic effect.

Whatever promotes the conscious and the unconscious working together can be part of a scene. If poetry, music, drawings, photos or dreams make it easier to release repressed memories, put them into your quest and other scenes or attach them to what you've written.

SIX

The Yellow Stage, Acceptance

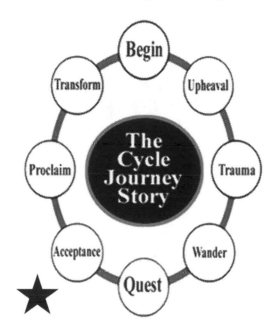

New Realizations

"Things do not change; we do.
If one advances confidently in the direction of one's dreams,
And endeavors to live the life which one has imagined,
One will meet with a success unexpected in common hours."
~Henry David Thoreau, Author, Poet

An Introduction To Stage Six

It's shocking and at the same time thrilling that there are so many new possibilities in your life. Your world has changed. You're different. Accepting the results of a quest requires you look deeply inside yourself.

Contemplation, giving your full attention to considering the results of the quest is the main theme in the Essentials. Your Deeper Insight is about your egos changing relationship to the Self. The novel *Under the Tuscan Sun* and the movies *Something's Gotta Give* and *It's Complicated* present different sides of acceptance. What's more Humpty Dumpty isn't the same unchangeable egg and our scenes show us struggling to shed our old images.

Stage Six finishes with Tell * Journal * Write coaching where you'll be challenged to referee a debate between your inner critic and inner advocate.

The Essentials

Everyone has internal dialogue, an inner discussion whether we should do this or stop doing that, a vote for one thing and against another. We spend our lives struggling to select from the better of two options. In a few situations, in our wisest place we discover a middle road, a way to have the best of both worlds by mixing two choices.

Imagine what it's like to be a knight returned from a successful quest. You've rescued the damsel, slayed the dragon or fought the battle against what you once believed to be an unbeatable foe. **You've been tested and the ordeal changed you at the deepest level.**

Many of your likes and dislikes have been remixed, sometimes in ways you're unprepared for. The way you use your time shifts as you adjust the importance attached to different parts of life. Your circle of friends isn't the same. Clothes, taste in foods, entertainment you prefer, and what you call home might change. The quest is complete and you're aware of your full potential and have settled on a new destiny.

Acceptance is an act of inner contemplation, focusing the mind's attention on what's necessary to fully come to terms with expected and unexpected quest results. The quester faces the clash of the new and old worlds, two choices, and needs to find a way to restructure life and create a new balance, a truer reality.

There is a deliberative quality to this contemplative recognition. You need to think creatively about what has come out of the quest. **This meditative, conscious/unconscious view is a dialogue with your inner wisdom necessary to accept the trueness and authenticity of the quest results.**

When quest thoughts come, which they will, don't try to make them go away. Return your attention to the meditative in and out flow of your breath. Think of two calming words like peace and harmony. Relax and listen to the rhythm of your breath. Much of the time it will feel like nothing is happening. Other times, the mind quiets and you seem to enter a profound silence. Sit and let the acceptance process evolve in any way it wants.

Thoughts from your unconscious come without encouragement. You might embrace mindfulness, paying conscious attention to the sensations of the body and letting your acceptance feelings drift through those sensations or you may sit in a chair and simply focus on the breath as it moves in and out. You'll be able to examine quest perceptions and notions without having them control you or being controlled by them.

After meditating on the acceptance of quest results, you'll often have answers to questions about your Cycle Journey float into your mind. This is the expanded awareness you need for full quest acceptance. You'll feel new inner peace and an assurance your quest was precisely the one you needed to claim your destiny, and you'll feel confident you're ready to proclaim your quest to the world.

Active imagination, internal communication like this takes careful thought and a committed consideration of all the aspects of the quest. Your examination leads to the realization a new destiny requires adjustments in every area of life, some uncomplicated and some more challenging.

Your new understanding is likely to be accompanied by the appearance of an unconscious inner critic. This judge or faultfinder, which insists it's trying to help you with its cautions and warnings, points out weaknesses and shortcomings. It claims it wants to aid you in adapting to a new quest's perils. Its power lies in knowing every past difficulty repressed in your shadow.

You won't have to wait to hear rationales for being cautious about accepting the quest results. It uses justifications like, "think this through," or "your new ideas may be too hard and you should have more preparation." Critic warnings and cautions might include, "What happens if you fail?" "Think about all the people you'll disappoint," "You shouldn't move so fast." or "Don't make big changes you'll regret later."

Expect the advice you get to be full of the limiting **should** and even more restrictive, **shouldn't**. They're the favorite cautions of the inner critic. Their power lies in an ability to call upon your sense of duty and propriety. They tug at your belief that you must still do what you've always thought to be the right thing.

This internal critic made its first appearance in childhood when parents, relatives, friends, and teachers imposed limitations and restrictions. These judgmental, duty-oriented and often well-intentioned commands kept in your shadow give **should** and **shouldn't** power. The critic is your unconscious making its way into the conscious. It presents reasons why you should pull back, slow down or stop completely.

Just as dark and light, yes and no, and young and old are opposites, in acceptance there needs to be a counter to the inner critic, an inner advocate, a true believer in your potential. This supporter has enthusiasm and a proponent's beliefs about what's been accomplished and what can be accomplished. It can insist, "Look what you've done," "you are good enough, and you succeeded in your quest and there's no limit to what you can do." **Can** and **could** are ideal counters to the inner critic's **should** and **shouldn't** and make it clear the quest has taught you how much ability, skill, and willpower you can apply to taking your quest into the world. The advocate wants to push forward, move faster and try new things.

Obviously imagined communication between the critic urging you to pull back and the advocate urging you to push forward is never heard by anyone but you. **It's active imagination internal dialogue, a push/ pull deliberation with the pluses and minuses or the strong and weak points of the quest results running through your mind.** This necessary interaction of creativity, imagination, and intuition puts unconscious inner wisdom to its best use. It employs well-practiced strategies of the opposing energies in your unconscious. If you are to have the courage to proclaim quest results to the wider world, you need to experience the frustration of letting this internal communication, the struggle of opposites, play out.

Both the critic and the advocate have points you want to take into account, and neither is totally in the right. Each has views you need to hear and each believes they have your best interests at heart. If you are to gain a balanced view of your quest results, patience is required to resolve their tension and make use of these opposing energies.

The critic expresses necessary caution, thoughtfulness, and restraint. It knows your shortcomings and limitations and keeps you from getting swept up in the moment and plunging over a cliff and helps avoid being overzealous.

On the other hand the advocate, your champion and defender, is equally vital in achieving the best possible quest outcomes. It presents strengths and talents and makes a case for you to move forward. When it comes to your potential, it's the holder of confidence, belief, and self-reliance.

You need the mix of advice from a sensible critic and an enthusiastic advocate to make your dreams come true. To get this blending there is a third approach to the critic and advocate, a way to combine the talents of both. You strive to interpret their input so you achieve a situational balance between the two. This middle view gets the best out of these opposing energies by being open to creativity and imagination and relying on your intuition to guide you.

This is where you develop a sense of the critic's and the advocate's polarity. When their opposite properties or powers are taken into account, you gain a deeper understanding of your options for realizing your immediate needs. In some situations the critic needs to come to the forefront, possibly in a dangerous or difficult time, and other times the advocate becomes your champion and takes the lead, perhaps when there is a fear of doing or trying something new. In a few situations what's needed is a balance of both their talents.

To make the best use of your internal critic and advocate learn the techniques that take their dialogue to a higher level.

- **Avoid the pronoun *I*.** In every critic and advocate dialogue use your name—"Sylvia, your quest is too hard," or "Court, you're not prepared for all you'll have to do," create distance from the Self and feel less personally threatened. Look for the way names are used in Sylvia's and Court's scenes.
- **Write out an imagined dialogue and don't be afraid to edit what you've put on paper.** This moves the inner critic and advocate out of your head and into the non-imaginary world. The sharper you make their dialogue, the more useful it will be.
- **Once you have a dialogue that represents your quest feelings, one that is a mix of the critic and advocate, read it out loud.**

Hearing your critic and advocate makes them real and creates a better balance between the two.

There will always be a natural friction, unrest and imbalance between the critic and the advocate. **This tension of opposites takes time, patience, and practice to master and comes with frustration and exasperation.**

However we view the communication, acceptance embraces a viewpoint which pushes us forward toward a new destiny. Lionel Corbett's *Psyche and the Sacred* suggests an approach to integrating acceptance into life. "Surrender means allowing life to happen rather than opposing the flow of life. Accepting the present moment without resistance, we simply do what needs to be done without labeling the situation as good or bad according to the ego's criteria."

Under the Tuscan Sun is an acceptance novel. After a divorce Frances Mayes buys a Tuscan villa in need of a complete renovation. Her inner critic has a fit when she gives into this impulse. She struggles to accept her new life, the Italian way of doing things, and chances for romance. For a time she wishes she'd paid more attention to her inner critic when it warned her of possible villa and personal disasters. Each challenge and the shifting relationship between her opposing energies pushes her closer to creating new balance in her life.

First Frances' critic and advocate must learn to work together to help her acknowledge her Tuscan quest has brought about a new reality filled with challenges and an altered destiny. Her admission can be centered on a reassessment, reframing, and recognition of a new calling based on what she knows deep inside—it took considerable ability and commitment to make her villa and herself whole again. She begins by reevaluating her personal limitations, restrictions no longer in line with the person who has begun the restoration—she learns to push forward. What's more Frances has an expanded awareness. The unique identity of the Tuscan villa lets her and her inner advocate come up with a change-oriented view of how she rebuilt her life.

Frances accepts she has made a new home in Italy. Her rebuilt villa becomes a metaphor for a new life. To acknowledge her inner critic and strengthen her inner advocate's confidence, she tells others, Italian friends and people from her old life despite considerable obstacles she did the nearly impossible and created a new life at the same time.

Two Nancy Meyer movies *Something's Gotta Give* and *It's Complicated* present contrasting views of how acceptance works in relationships. In *Something's Gotta Give,* after a heart attack, Harry Sanborn, Jack Nicholson, a confirmed bachelor, struggles until near the end of the movie to accept he loves Erica Barry, Dianne Keaton. Meyer's companion movie, *It's Complicated*, is the other side of the acceptance coin. Jane Alder, Meryl Streep, and her ex-husband, Jake Alder, have an affair where Jane finally accepts she can let go of Jake and move on with her life.

One of Jane's lessons in *It's Complicated* is letting go of limiting judgements based on an old belief she isn't good enough, can't make a successful marriage work and needs to pull back. The affair gives her inner advocate the ammunition it needs to see she no longer loves her ex-husband and it's time to learn from her past marriage and move on or push forward.

In *Something's Gotta Give* for most of his life Harry Sanborn's inner critic used his string of affairs to tell him he's not capable of having a lasting relationship and needs to pull back whenever a woman gets too serious. At the end of the movie, on a bridge in Paris, after he has undertaken a quest to review his past relationships, he faces the inner critic and uses his inner advocate to silence his old belief. He tells Erica Barry, "Turns out the heart attack was easy to get over. You... were something else. I finally get it. I'm 63 years old... and I'm in love for the first time in my life."

Part of acceptance success is realizing criticism or resistance to change, a feeling you need to pull back, is a warning the dialogue between the inner critic and inner advocate isn't complete. It's your task to find a way to bring necessary balance to their communication.

There are established critic strategies which delay this balance.

Denial is the unwillingness, despite obvious facts, to accept any quest achievements capable of upsetting your inflexible view of the world. Denial skews success to the point where it is remembered as not being totally successful. What you thought you did is an illusion. You didn't look carefully, there's no real truth to any of your quest results.

Rationalization gives the inner critic acceptable reasons for unacceptable thoughts or actions, such as ignoring quest results entirely. It's the wrong quest for you, or it doesn't make any difference what you think you achieved and nothing will change are seductive rationalizations. Even though they don't make sense, these emotional justifications make turning back and abandoning acceptance of quest results seem like a logical decision. This is where your advocate needs strong beliefs and the facts to debunk the clever enticements of the inner critic.

Projection happens when the critic uses feelings or intentions beginning within us and assigns them to another person—it's my wife who wants me to stop, or my boss wouldn't want me to do this or she's to blame or he's at fault. The fear of acceptance and unwillingness to meet the challenge of change is behind this inner critic projection. Once your advocate is aware of the deception, the projection can be rejected and the advocate is free to put forward a factual reality interpretation.

In her book, *Radical Acceptance*, Dr. Tara Brach indirectly makes the case for the inner advocate's ability to see our lives as they really are. "Radical Acceptance reverses our habit of living at war with experiences that are unfamiliar, frightening or intense. It is the antidote to years of neglecting ourselves, years of judging and treating ourselves harshly, years of rejecting this moment's experience. Radical Acceptance is the willingness to experience ourselves and our life as it is…As we free ourselves from the suffering of 'something is wrong with me,' we trust and express the fullness of who we are." Dr. Brach stresses Radical Acceptance isn't a type of resignation and doesn't make us passive when she writes, "Carl Jung describes the spiritual path as an unfolding into *wholeness*…we embrace life in all it realness—broken, messy, mysterious and vibrantly alive. To paraphrase Jung, you understand with acceptance you've taken a step closer to claiming your individuation."

Try this exercise with your critic and advocate. Pick something you'd like to accomplish, something with a built in risk—lose weight, go on a trip, buy a new house or go back to school. First write the critic's view, every carefully thought out reason why you should pull back. Be hard on yourself. Imagine the worst possible consequences. Now play the inner advocate. Answer the inner critic. Write responses to every objection and limiting criticism. Compare the inner critics and the inner advocate's sheets. If they seem out of balance revise the answers.

Work on the replies until you're sure you've made them as strong as you can and you've created a new equilibrium, a combination of the best of the critic and the advocate's advice. Now you can push forward without reservation. **Out of this tension of opposites balanced answers have allowed deeper acceptance.**

This Active Imagination exercise strengthens the unconscious/conscious connection to the point where the inner critic and the inner advocate naturally form a partnership with a goal of moving toward your transformation.

Stage 6 Deeper Insight

The Ego

"So far as we know, consciousness is always ego-consciousness. In order to be conscious of myself, I must be able to distinguish myself from others. Relationships can only take place where this distinction exists." ~C. G. Jung

The ego often blocks the introspection necessary for acceptance. It's an organized conscious mediator between you and reality, especially when it functions both in perception and adaptation to life. It organizes thoughts and intuitions, feelings, and sensations, has access to unrepressed memories and can see acceptance as a stability threat. The ego's place at the junction between the inner and outer worlds makes it an inner traffic cop responsible for the opinion you have about yourself.

The ego, the subject of the conscious, comes into existence made up partly by inherited disposition, your basic character, and partly by unconsciously acquired impressions. The ego is the central complex in the conscious and it contains our awareness of an existing and continuing sense of personal identity. It provides a sense of consistency and direction in conscious life. It opposes what threatens the delicate consciousness and works to convince us to plan and analyze our experience. The ego has no unconscious elements. Its only conscious contents are derived from personal experience.

In upheaval before we know how to tap into inner wisdom we look to the ego for direction. Conscious world experience may have no answer for our turmoil. We struggle to find a voice for the inner pain we feel. With no adequate answer we wander, looking for some conscious experience which provides a way to express the chaos the upheaval has brought to our life.

The quest may be the first time we have ever relied on guidance from the Self and looked deeper, peered into the depths of the unconscious world. In this relationship there is a power shift and the ego begins to take direction from the Self.

At quest's end there's a need for a rebalancing, a deeper acceptance of all the implications of the quest results. Now, as the ego follows the Self's direction, there is a readiness to move back into the world with a balanced view that shifts to wholeness. We can listen to inner wisdom and adapt to outer world experiences. With acceptance in place, the next step of relating to the outer world in a new and different way becomes proof of readiness for change.

The Stories For Stage Six

<u>Humpty's Scene Six:</u>

A New View

Humpty no longer sees himself as the unexciting hatchery
worker who wore his black frock coat to work every day.

<u>Court's Scene Six:</u>

Inspiration

So many strange creatures, wouldn't it be incredible
to see them alive and in one place, a kind of creature
world where they'd been mysteriously exiled.

<u>Sylvia's Scene Six:</u>

A Dream Comes True

I'll never forget looking in the mirror, squaring my shoulders,
winking at my image and saying, "I've gotten to the right place."

<u>Your Cycle Journey Story:</u>

Scene Six - Acceptance

Humpty's Story Continues:
Chapter Six: A New View

"Finish my quest, be an example for every young egg." So he'll never forget how uncommon his life has become, Humpty begins each day repeating that mantra. He's taking online courses his friend Honker recommended and his work with young eggs has generated praise from scores of egglet parents.

Eggs have come up to his wife, rubbed their shell's against hers and gone on and on about how Humpty has changed their young egg's life. The school his egglets attend called and asked Humpty to speak to their teachers on his work. His egglet, Doodle, who had been so embarrassed over her father's appearance, is always asking to bring her friends over so they can meet her famous father and touch his cracks and missing pieces.

Ovum College read about his youth program and set aside their age requirement so they could offer him a scholarship. Yesterday he received a letter from one of the king's Faberge egg ministers. It read, "I've mentioned your great fall at court and the brave way you've handled yourself. King Crumpets told me to tell you, 'Jolly good show, you're an example to every other egg in the kingdom.'" Last Tuesday, for the entire day Humpty didn't once think about his damaged shell.

With scores of campers depending on him for guidance not a minute can be wasted. To keep up with his charges, he's started to get up early and do exercises to strengthen the proteins in his yolk. On most days he's so preoccupied with the young eggs and their problems his shell and his old hatchery job never enters his mind. Almost every night he stays up late studying for his college exams and sketching out new camper programs—he feels years younger and senses his white bubbling with new life and his yoke pulsating with creative energy.

Sometimes late at night he recalls his pre-fall life. There are parts of his previous existence he misses. Occasionally he hears a critical voice coming from deep in his yoke. "Humpty, admit you've moved too fast and won't be able to keep up with all the changes. Back before the terrible tumble everything in life was predictable. You got your paycheck on the last Friday of the month and knew what everyone, even your boss, thought of you. That's the way a good egg should live."

That's when another, more optimistic voice fills the inside of his shell. "Humpty Dumpty, don't listen to that foolishness. You may be losing some certainty, but before the fall your life had no excitement or challenges. Face it, you were bored. Today you have a chance to be a better egg than you ever imagined possible."

The critical voice returns. "Working with egglet campers is too uncertain. Humpty, at the camp you don't even know if you'll get paid. What's more your yoke bubbles every time you think about speaking to the parents of young eggs, and if that's not enough, your college courses are so hard they could fry you."

Humpty tries to blot out the voices by twirling in circles. Only a few months ago he'd tied his success to his gleaming shell. Today that self-absorption seems unimaginable. For the first time, as scary as it is, he's in charge of his life and doing something of great consequence, work which can make the egg kingdom a better place.

It comes to him that counseling the young egglets had always been his authentic destiny, his true place in the kingdom. He's found a life path he can follow. He shudders as he realizes for the first time the old Humpty, who subsisted on the oohs and ayahs his gleaming shell attracted, can never be reclaimed.

He understands both the critical and cheerleader voices that came into his head had something to say. His life is uncertain and at the same time it's filled with excitement and new variety.

He senses his place in the egg universe has been remixed. With the excitement comes the fear he won't be up to meeting the new challenges. His motivation will have to come from a deeper feeling of accomplishment he'll get from watching the success of the young eggs he's helped.

Humpty takes great comfort in his vision of an endless supply of young egglets to counsel. He stares into the mirror, runs his hands over the cracks and the spots where there are missing pieces of shell. After the great fall, he'd been so self-conscious about his unsmooth look. Today he's gained a new awareness and accepts his less than perfect shell as a sign he's tapped into a deeper wisdom. The truth is the challenge of dealing with the cracks and missing pieces have revealed a depth of character he never knew existed. He says out loud, "I understand and accept the course of my life has changed. A few things I thought I cared about have been lost, but so much more has been gained."

Court's Scene Six

Inspiration

On a gray February day I started my lesson on how acceptance and personal viewpoint worked to change my world view.

The doctor examined the x-rays, held them up to the light, peered over his glasses and shook his head the way a television doctor would before he tells you that you have an incurable disease. "Mr. Johnson, both hips are shot, its bone on bone and you're going to need to have them replaced."

Over the next three months, without any complications, I had the surgery on the left and right hips. Under the best circumstances rehab takes the patience of a saint, which is a trait that has eluded me. Somehow, along with enough grouching for ten people, I made it.

Ask anyone who's had a joint replacement and they'll tell you there's one strange side effect to becoming part bionic; it takes time to get back to a normal sleep pattern. For months I awoke at three o'clock in the morning and knew I wouldn't go back to sleep until the next afternoon. It seemed like a perfect opportunity to write.

Each night for the week after I came home from the hospital I banged away at the keyboard. Before I went to bed I'd read over what I'd wrote. Most of it barely made sense.

My focus seemed to have vanished. In the middle of the night sitting alone in my study, sometimes I imagined hearing dad's badgering, critical voice. "You've waited too long to start this silly writing career. Can't you see this is a young man's game? It'll be like the band. As soon as it gets too hard you'll quit."

I thought back to aimless days after my divorce and all my random jobs. For once maybe dad had it right. I had waited too long and I'd never be able to escape my past. I tried reading, but the uninterrupted silence and creepy shadows made me jumpy.

Early on a Friday morning, three weeks after my operations and past my need for mind dulling pain medication, with another jazz favorite, Charlie Parker playing a sax solo in the background, I absentmindedly leafed through an old mythology book, what's called a *Bestiary*, with pictures of mythical creatures and comments on their moral significance. So many strange creatures, wouldn't it be incredible to see them alive and in one place, a kind of creature world where they'd been mysteriously exiled.

I'm not sure how long I stared before the idea came charging out of my unconscious so completely formed I dropped the book. Suppose a creature world really existed on a mysterious island. The hero of the story would somehow get to the world and explore it. After ten pages I knew the story could work.

The creature world inspiration, bringing mythical creatures to life, giving them backstories, personality, and ancient rivalries could be the key to letting go of the restrictions I'd put on myself. I'd make this my opportunity to adopt a new viewpoint and a fresh writing style.

For weeks I kept my creature world a secret. I'd go to bed, hardy able to wait for three o'clock to come again. Over a few weeks, new characters were developed. Fifteen-year-old Napoleon Prince, the main character would have dreams about a fabulous world full of mythic creatures like harpies, hellhounds, goblins, trolls and the most dangerous of all, the hydra. One day, as if his dream had come alive, deep in the woods he steps through a green mist and finds himself on the creature island.

I imagined my inner critic's no-nonsense voice. "Courtney Johnson, I'm using your full name to make you face facts. You're no Tolkien and this story isn't going to be the next Lord of the Rings. Your plot is too complex. You don't know enough mythology to bring a mythical world to life. Your other stories didn't make the grade. Why should you expect this one to be different?"

My champion's voice came into my head. "So what if you're not Tolkien. You can make the plot simpler and you can learn the mythology. Just let yourself believe it's a great story."

I saw the critic as less of a threat and more as a voice warning me of possible trouble spots, and I knew my champion's suggestions would require a big revision. There'd been a rebalancing in the relationship between my critic and advocate and I understood I could make use of input from both.

A couple of weeks later I had sixty pages and at least as much research on mythical creatures. This felt like my storytelling sweet spot, a mythical fantasy world, the Creature Exile World, where I could put my main character into every imaginable type of danger.

Time flew by and in spite of waking at three o'clock and never getting more than five hours sleep I didn't feel tired. New characters and different plot possibilities sprang up every night. I had a hundred pages and a vision of the final scene where Napoleon battled the hydra.

Friends, casual acquaintances, clerks in stores and waiters and waitresses, anyone who would listen heard about my Exile World novel. They all seemed interested, some even fascinated.

Any time you go public you run into packs of real-life critics and faultfinders who are waiting to pounce on you. "A writer at your age, come on." "Why aren't you published?" The real-life critics had good points. I am older than most people who start a writing career and I hadn't been published. Some of the criticisms got me off course until I figured everyone has obstacles they have to overcome. Along the way I lost a few friends, but gained more new ones.

By now I had two-hundred pages of the story, which I'd named *Napoleon Prince and The Creature Exile World*. My hero had allies, Vikings who have been trapped in the world for a thousand years. The plot had subplots, battles and a love story.

I joined a new writers group, got feedback and took all kinds of chances with the plot and characters. One night it came to me, the chance to be a storyteller is the destiny I'd always wanted and now there were no excuses. It's like the old saying, when you get what you want, you've got to want what you get.

In the Napoleon Prince adventure I'd managed to combine fantasy and science fiction and propose that many myths could have alien origins.

Like a little kid looking at a toy catalogue, I became one-dimensional. All I wanted to do was go over dialogue, plot strategies and polish settings. I had fellow writers I e-mailed regularly. More and more my old life seemed dreamlike.

My three-hundred page *Napoleon Prince and The Creature Exile World* book got finished. The relationship between my critic and advocate evolved. By the end of the book I could see they'd reached some kind of a peace accord based on the realization they needed each other. The critic pulled me back when I got outside my capabilities and the advocate stepped in to push forward when I lost my way. I'd learned to see them as close allies I'd be lost without.

One insight about having my hips redone shook me up. On the inside I could lay claim to being a new person. There was me before the operation and me after the operation, and dad didn't have any power over the new me. It's a weird, overly creative interpretation and maybe my critic, advocate and the hips connection didn't rate as anything more than a flight of fantasy. Who cares, destiny had its own agenda and its own way of getting to the truth. Besides you can't be a writer unless you believe you can make the imaginary real.

STITCHING – <u>Connecting Scenes Six and Seven:</u>

The creature world book jolted my reality. I'd found something I loved to do and I didn't have room for dad's naysayer comments. He gradually disappeared into whatever dark mist he called home.

New writing skills magically appeared. I sensed I'd gotten to be a good writer. My first rejection letters drove home the point good isn't good enough. Writing is the same as patching holes in a dyke. Plug up one, fix a weakness, and for a while your story looks perfect, like it'll hold forever.

You start to think your one step away from a bestseller. A new leak opens, a story weakness rears its ugly head and story problems are everywhere. The better you get the more you understand new leaks are going to pop up every day.

In spite of the obstacles, through thick and thin and revision after revision I kept at it. Only once, after some especially brutal feedback, did I almost give up.

Sylvia's Scene Six

A Dream Comes True

The catalogue had dozens of choices and I could begin with any four. For two weeks I'd gone over the list, reading and rereading the course descriptions and agonizing over which ones to take first. I cut to twenty-five then it took a sleepless night to pare down to ten. The next six had me on pins and needles. In one week I changed my mind at least twenty times.

Early on a Friday morning I stared at the paper for a minute, picked up a red pencil, gritted my teeth and circled four courses—the first, Death and Dying: A Metaphysical View, two, the Unified Field: Modern Theoretical Physics Meets Ancient Metaphysics, number three, Great Spiritual Masters and Teachers, and four, Awaking to the True Self. Those courses, when I enrolled at a spiritual-based university, became a dividing line and allowed me to accept myself in a place far from my usual world.

The day I went to the mailbox and found the Awaking to the True Self course I felt my passion for learning, which struggled through four marriages to be heard and understood, had been set free. That night I stayed up reading through the material until I fell asleep. At the end of a couple of weeks I took my first exam and got a perfect score. I looked in the mirror, squared my shoulders, winked at my image and said, "I've gotten to the right place."

My excitement, joy, happiness and sense of being on a new path plunged me forward. The years of middle of the night studying and cramming flew by as I worked my way through course after course. At the end came my dissertation on *The Dark Night Journey, Answering Destiny's Call*.

This is where my inner critic made an appearance. "Sylvia, pull back, slow down. You've done OK writing short papers, taking quizzes and writing your thesis. A Ph.D. dissertation, hold on. You'll be up against real scholars and they'll know you're not ready."

For weeks I swayed back and forth. The imaginary judgmental voice sounded like it had my best interests at heart. Maybe the voice had a point. I might have gone too far too fast. Higher education could be beyond me.

A confident voice, my inner defender made a sudden appearance. "You've got the grades. Everything you've done has been superior work. There's been praise from the faculty. This is the educational opportunity you've always dreamed about."

My imaginary advocate had a calm, self-assured way of overriding old critical messages. That didn't mean I stopped working extra-hard. The inner critic had good points. This was my first attempt at writing a dissertation. I needed an original viewpoint.

It took several months to do the research, go through my experiences and tie everything into how the Dark Night impacted individuals in today's world. I studied C. G. Jung's theory of individuation. It fit my Self-discovery process and was natural for me to incorporate into the Cycle Journey. Whatever obstacles showed up didn't matter, nothing would stop me from completing my paper.

The other sign of a long-lasting commitment to my education came when I made space for my own office. I bought a desk, a laptop, a printer and a bookcase I could fill with new books which reflected my growing insistence I would master the Dark Night and the Dark Night of the Soul and how the process can transform a person. My new office became a symbol to my evolving commitment to learning.

The praise I received from the faculty and the president made my graduation special. I felt I'd been welcomed to a new community excited about education, self-discovery and spiritual growth.

I moved on, taking more classes, including Spiritual Psychology at another distance learning university.

After writing my dissertation the relationship with my inner critic changed. Its advice seemed calmer, almost like I'd gained its respect. There were still cautions and don't go too fast warnings, but they were never again threatening or full of predictions of doom.

My new life path reached a deeper level in a six month Psyche and The Sacred dream work group taught by a Jungian Analyst. Dr. Lionel Corbett. He arranged us in a circle, discussed our dreams, and lectured on the timeless psychological topics that allowed me to gain an understanding of my life and the changes I needed to make.

His way of explaining being open to the encouragement of the Self's inner wisdom, rather than wanting to please the ego, and following a spiritual connection not under our control changed how I live my life.

Individuation, the conscious, ego, unconscious, shadow, and Self are the components of a view on how I can transform my life.

Whether it's a paper, teaching a class, or writing a book, there are no limits on what I can accomplish as long as that creativity, imagination and intuition comes from my inner wisdom, what I now call Self.

STITCHING – <u>Connecting Scenes Six and Seven:</u>

Learning is like breathing—I need it to survive. The belief in one's Self and one's inner power had been the most elusive quality in my life. Over the years the disasters and downturns chipped away at my faith in myself. School and a thirst for knowledge rebuilt my self-image. For me destiny has always been intertwined with Self-discovery. I felt a deep inner calling to share my hard earned wisdom with others.

Tell * Journal * Write

Scene Six

Coaches get you to look deep inside yourself. Scene six, acceptance, shows you're making time for contemplation and deliberation. You'll work on a growing trust between the conscious and unconscious and come up with a way to proclaim your new destiny.

You've learned acceptance is where your **inner critic and inner advocate** make an appearance. Your scene needs a constructive dialogue between these opposing parts of your unconscious. They have important views, but neither should dominate the scene. You'll write how you've used the best of those differing outlooks to reach a new understanding about the authentic destiny you found in the quest.

Don't fall into the trap of seeing the critic as threatening and the advocate as your unabashed champion. Instead try to represent the best and most reasonable parts of the inner critic and advocate. Listen and choose the most helpful feedback, the points which move you toward successful acceptance of your quest destiny.

Acknowledge the quest results and bring together the past and the present. Begin the scene by establishing your personal view in one of the first paragraphs. Are you afraid, excited, angry, confused, thrilled, or panicked? As acceptance takes hold your view can change or evolve to curious, happy, or calm. In scene six Court reached a crossroad in viewing himself as a writer. "On a gray February day I started my lesson on how acceptance and personal viewpoint work together to change the way I looked at the world."

If you can establish your view in the opening paragraphs, the rest of the scene will flow naturally. In Sylvia's scene six she says, "Those courses, when I enrolled at a spiritual-based university, became a dividing line and allowed me to accept myself in a place far from my usual world."

Backstory, past events influence the way you and everyone else behave. Court imagines what his father might say about his writing. "You've waited too long to start this writing career. Can't you see this is a young man's game? Besides, you might as well admit it'll be just like the band. As soon as it gets too hard you'll quit."

Instead of being angry or discouraged, Court needs to take the advice to heart. He has waited until he is older to start writing. His age does make his new career more of a challenge—but far from being an insurmountable obstacle. Sooner or later he may be tempted to quit. He doesn't have to give into the temptation. Instead he can reframe the inner critic warnings into helpful cautions.

Add to backstory in small bits, no more than a paragraph at a time. Include only what's necessary to understand how your history or your families' history influenced the scene. In her scene six Sylvia wrote, "My passion for learning, which struggled through four marriages to be heard and understood, had been set free."

Backstory is an essential part of building deeper understanding into the scene. You can add pieces of backstory after you've written the scene. A deeper look at the past provides the context needed to see your life as more than a series of isolated incidents.

Acceptance is often an emotional rollercoaster. Let your five senses and your sixth sense show your sway of feelings and emotions. Sight, smell, sound, taste and touch create vivid mental images.

- Don't let what you see dominate scenes.
- Aromas, odors, and scents make it easier for you to speak with few words.
- Sound, even silence, as much as shouting, whispering, foot-tapping and banging, can be a part of a vivid description that puts tension in a scene.
- Taste, eating and drinking, even kissing or tasting sweat and freezing air brings primal memories to life.
- Touch is filled with pleasure or pain. A metaphor or simile, his beard felt like sandpaper, brings touch to life.

Acceptance needs your sixth sense, the inner place not bound by old prejudices or rigid rules. Intuition or instinct, creativity and inspiration along with imagination coupled with vision are the parts of the sixth sense that connect to the unconscious.

Intuition puts instincts in play. It is our direct perception or keen insights of deep creative awareness nercessary to implement quest results. When Sylvia says, "My imaginary advocate had a calm, self-assured way of overriding old critical messages," she's really talking about listening to her intuition.

Creativity comes from inspirations which bring ideas, innovative forms, and novel interpretations into acceptance reality.

Imagination is the visionary talent which forms quest images or concepts not actually perceived by the senses.

Words to use in your acceptance scene are:

Contemplation	Energies	Judgmental
Acknowledge	Belief	Life Path
Recognition	Champion	Shortcomings
Examination	New Viewpoint	No Limits
No Limits	Proponent	Destiny's Agenda

The key deeper insight and expanded awareness which comes out of acceptance is the knowledge the imagined internal dialogue between the critic and advocate is a necessary interaction if acceptance is to be made at a balanced level.

SEVEN

The Orange Stage, Proclaim

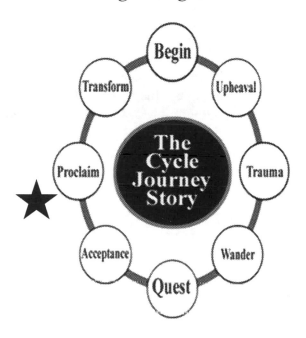

Wishes Come True

"If you do follow your bliss you put yourself on a kind of
track that has been there all the while, waiting for you,
and the life that you ought to be living is the one you are
living. Follow your bliss and don't be afraid, and doors
will open where you didn't know they were going to be."

~Joseph Campbell, Author, Philosopher and Teacher

An Introduction To Stage Seven

To march into the world and tell everyone about your authentic destiny is a scary challenge. The key to your success and the way you prepare for approval and disapproval is continuing to work with your inner critic and inner advocate.

Once you have an understanding of proclaiming essentials you'll see how Franklin Roosevelt won the 1932 presidency by mastering proclaiming and discover how a teenage boy, in the movie *Saint Ralph*, uses proclaiming to change his and his mother's life. The persona, the face you show the world, is the ideal Deeper Insight for proclaiming. Humpty Dumpty is doing interviews with The Egg Timer Magazine and taking on his harshest critic, The Big Egg, and we're dealing with feedback from critics and supporters.

In Stage Seven's Tell * Journal * Write coaching segment you'll learn about the importance of creativity and imagination in proclaiming and get tips on using setting and props in your writing.

The Essentials

You've gotten past your own internal dialogue. It's time to deal with the many and varied opinions you'll face when you take a new destiny into the world. Don't underestimate this test. **More Cycle Journeys are stopped in proclaiming than any other stage.**

Your view may be, "I've done it. I've made it through the hardest part of my Cycle Journey. I've worked with my opposites, the inner critic and inner advocate and accepted the changes I've made in my life. It's time to tell everyone the exciting news."

When it comes to believing changes we think are wonderful will be viewed the same way by everyone in the wider world, most of us have a childlike innocence. How could anyone think the new you along with your freshly discovered authentic destiny isn't wonderful?

You've prepared for this proclaiming. The inner critic and the inner advocate have communicated and acceptance won the day. It's time to push on. You'll let others know about an expanded awareness and share a true and incorruptible calling. You're positive your beliefs are strong enough to bring your quest results into the wider world.

Family, friends, coworkers, and acquaintances need to know these exciting changes. Some people will be enthusiastic, even thrilled new horizons have opened up in your life. There also may be resistance and outright opposition. Outer critics will want you to pull back. It can be a shock to be bubbling with passion about a life-changing quest and find friends, business associates or even those closest to you assuming the outer critic role and letting you know they're not overjoyed about the new possibilities in your life.

The announcement of the changes you've made needs careful thought. Before you proclaim, pick out who's with you, who's excited about the new possibilities and who's a critic full of objections and resisting the changes you're making. Prepare to do close listening. There will be tension and frustration as you attempt to live with these divergent views and come up with a perspective combining the best of the contrasting opinions on your quest.

Before you take on the outer critics and advocates you can proclaim by example. A trip to a foreign country, taking a course and getting a certification, even exhibiting a painting or having a concert can be part of your outreach. In the movie *Saint Ralph*, a teenage boy, Ralph Walker, an outcast among his classmates, trains for the 1954 Boston Marathon and hopes a victory will be the proclaiming his mother needs to awaken from a coma. After a close race, he wins second place and gives the medal to his mother who then wakes up.

It's important to wait for the right time for proclaiming a new destiny. Conrad Black's biography, *Franklin Delano Roosevelt, Champion of Freedom*, tells of a classic example about waiting for the right time to proclaim before the widest possible audience.

In 1921 at age thirty-nine during an August vacation at Campobello Island in Canada, after exercising Roosevelt came down with a fever which weeks later a doctor diagnosed as poliomyelitis.

His struggles with paralysis molded FDR as a man and a president. With the support of his wife, Eleanor, and his friend and political advisor, Louie Howe, and despite the wishes of his powerful critical mother that he pull back, Roosevelt waited to proclaim his readiness to move back into politics until he was sure he could deal with his disability. He won the 1928 race for governor of New York and the 1932 presidency.

The courage and maturity it took for FDR to execute his proclaiming with such skill can't be overstated. In the 1930's the disabled were commonly shunned by families, considered unemployable, and often put in asylums. Try to imagine Roosevelt's tension. He had to work to find the balance he needed, the mix of being aggressive and careful, to reenter public life. FDR had special braces made and used practiced techniques to minimize the visual impact of his paralysis. He found a spot between being too public and too private before he risked proclaiming to the United States and then to the world. He expressed his personal philosophy and a rallying cry he would use in World War II when he wrote, "The only thing we have to fear is fear itself—nameless, unreasoning, unjustified terror which paralyzes needed efforts to convert retreat into advance."

A planned proclaiming has two elements. First, the wisdom to reveal a new quest in bits and pieces. Tell it to those closest to you before you branch out—Roosevelt made no secret of his limitations with his children, wife, and close friends. Their positive encouragement formed the base for his moving proclaiming into the wider world.

Second, like Roosevelt have a proclaiming plan which allows you to be fearless. If the quest is going back to school, talk about a course you're taking, possibly even show the textbook to your family. If it's interviewing for a new job, mention one interview, not all the ones you have scheduled. Family members may already know about a quest, but pick only close friends, ones you know will support your new direction.

Don't expect applause or cheering. You already have a base, what you've learned from your inner critic and inner advocate. You need time to adjust to the different real world views you'll meet when you proclaim. Anticipate a variety of reactions, be prepared for opposition. Some people will love your plans. There will be doubters, the skeptical and those adamant critics who are bitterly opposed and will insist you pull back.

Take into account all the responses. Whether it's a critic or an advocate, actively listen to the different views. When the outer critic or advocate finishes, restate what you've heard with an emphasis on the most helpful points—"What you said about needing to go back to school to make my new career work makes a lot of sense." When you've heard from the majority of the critics and advocates, pick a view which represents the best mix of the opposing views of your quest results. Look at your critic and advocate communications as learning opportunities, chances to fine-tune your quest.

In acceptance you've come to some resolution of the inner critic and inner advocate stances. Review the way you've resolved these interactions. When you encounter an outer critic, use your acceptance knowledge as a basis for resolving what you hear from the outer world. **Select the ways you'll announce—web-site, Twitter, Linked-in, e-mail, phoning key friends, lunches, speeches and one-on-one meetings are possibilities.**

Initial disapproving reactions may produce stage fright, a growing fear of criticism, a tension you're not sure you can stand. Review your commitment to the quest. Your Cycle Journey hasn't been random roaming. You've planned and analyzed and didn't get to the proclaiming stage by accident. Part of bringing your new destiny to the world requires you have the patience to resolve opposing views.

To cope with this tension of different views, recognize it's not just your calling at stake. You're pursuing a vision, your dreams. You've individuated on the inside; now it's time to show your new wholeness to the outside world. Don't hold back on your excitement and passion. Repeat to yourself, **push forward, don't pull back, push forward, don't pull back.**

Stage 7 Deeper Insight

The Persona

"The Persona is a complicated system of relationships between individual consciousness and society, fittingly enough a kind of mask designed on one hand to make a definite impression upon others, and, on the other, to conceal the true nature of the individual." ~C. G. Jung

A stable persona is a requirement for proclaiming our new destiny to the outer world. It's the face we show, the character we play in life and how we relate to others. It's displayed in our clothes and symbols such as a car or jewelry. Persona, from the Latin meaning mask or false face, is a social facade that reflects our life role.

Our adaptation to childhood expectations is the base from which the persona grows. Maturity teaches us much of our social success is dependent on a well-functioning ego flexible enough to adapt to different situations. It's natural for the persona to carry personality traits experience has taught us are desirable, at the same time repressing what we believe are undesirable traits in the unconscious.

When the ego identifies with the persona we start to believe we are who we pretend to be. The persona is our mask, the way we package the ego. In his quest scene Court's writer's outfit was an exterior costume. Instead of realizing the work it would take to be an accomplished writer he focused on outer perfection. The instructor in pointing out, "I'm not sure if you have the depth of character to pull off a first-class story," let Court know clothes may express a persona, but they don't make a true writer.

After an upheaval we may use the persona as a defense against the world seeing we have suffered an earthquake-like shock. On the other hand, the persona may be so badly shaken that the face we present to the world is confused and sways between extremes.

By the proclaiming stage we become more aware of the persona's necessary social function and know it does not truly reflect who we are as an individual. As they move through the Cycle Journey, some travelers are challenged by the difficulty of leaving their old persona behind. This obstacle can leave major parts of their transformation distorted or unrecognized.

Real change is a type of independence from the persona and a deeper realization of our unique individuality. Although the persona is still a useful social tool, a type of compromise with the outside world, it is not an essential part of who we are.

The Stories For Stage Seven
Humpty's Scene Seven:

Egg Expert
In two weeks Humpty will speak before the Kingdom's Egg Parents Association.

Court's Scene Seven:
Critic Crap
"It's crap, nothing more than convoluted, confusing crap," Winfred didn't mince words.

Sylvia's Scene Seven:
Midnight Samurai
The guy looks so alive, intense and unafraid of the world.

Your Cycle Journey Story:
Scene Seven - Proclaim

Humpty's Story Continues:
Chapter Seven: Egg Expert

Funny and ironic is the way Humpty describes what's happened since the great fall. What he thought to be the darkest day of his life, turned out to be the beginning of an amazing adventure. In two weeks Humpty will be the keynote speaker at the Kingdom's Egg Parents Association. A reporter and a photographer from *Egg Timer Magazine* are coming in the morning, just after the rooster crows, to interview him about his upcoming talk. He's so nervous he can feel his egg white bubbling. Mrs. Dumpty has cleaned the carton from top to bottom and polished the egglets' shells until they're gleaming.

Rays of sunlight stream through the carton's front window when the reporter, an attractive robin's egg with stylish orange hair, and photographer, an extra-large turkey egg carrying a fancy camera, arrive. Humpty has notes listing the points he wants to make about starting an after-school program for young egglets at risk of being lured into deviled egg gangs.

Humpty realizes he's forgotten he'd promised Mrs. Dumpty that for the photos he'd put a few dabs of makeup on his cracks and the spots where he has missing pieces. There's no time. Besides he doesn't feel right covering up who he really is. He'll have to disappoint her. His appearance pales in comparison to the importance of making the points the *Egg Timer* needs to hear about how the kingdom could do a better job of raising its young eggs.

Two of the egglets show the reporter and photographer into the carton's living room. Pictures are taken and the interview begins. It only takes a few questions before Humpty becomes so enthusiastic about stating his mission with the young eggs that he's waving his hands and shouting as he paces back and forth. He shakes his finger at the ceiling and his voice booms. "Never, never forget each of our young eggs is different, special in their own way. It's my calling to give them a sense of how unique they are."

Two hours go by with Humpty proudly showing pictures of the campers and asking the reporter and photographer questions about ways they think young egg education could be improved. It's mid-morning when the reporter holds up her hand and gives him a serious look. "Mr. Dumpty I don't mean to embarrass you. What about your cracks and missing shell pieces, don't the campers make fun of you?"

Humpty laughs. "Cracks and missing pieces it's still me. The young eggs are too busy playing games to pay attention to my less-than-perfect exterior. Oh, every once in a while they'll tell me they don't know which is more cracked my stories or my shell."

The robin's egg reporter hugs Humpty and tells him, "You've been one of my most inspiring interviews, even better than the one-legged quail egg who sings opera. We'd like to put your picture on the magazine's cover."

An hour after the reporter and photographer leave there's a pounding on the front door. A few seconds later the egglets show Humpty's old boss from the hatchery, the scowling Big Egg, into the living room. He wastes no time in telling everyone in the Dumpty family why he came to the carton. "What's this foolishness I keep hearing about you spending time at the egglets camp? This isn't work for a grownup egg. Everyone at the hatchery is positively embarrassed at the way you're cavorting around with those youngsters."

At the back of the living room Humpty's egglets are hissing.

"Why?" Humpty asks. "Are you saying the kingdom shouldn't pay attention to young eggs? Have you forgotten they're our future?"

"I- I don't know, I never looked at it your way." The Big Egg shakes his shell. "Anyway, your coworkers at the hatchery miss you. Against my better judgment I've decided to take pity on you. We need someone to sweep up loose pieces of straw. The pay is next to nothing. At least you'll be able to tell your family you have a decent job."

The egglets are waving vases and lamps above their shells.

Before the situation deteriorates further, Humpty glares at his old boss. "I'm never coming back to the hatchery, working with the young eggs is where I can be the most benefit to the kingdom."

The Big Egg shakes his shell and backs up in the direction of the door. "Utter foolishness, just as I expected Humpty Dumpty has gone completely mad." His old boss sees the egglets ready to attack and runs out the front door.

The next month *Egg Timer Magazine* hits the newsstands. Humpty's picture, cracks and missing pieces is on the front cover. At the bottom of the page there's a comment on his wonderful sense of humor and the rugged good looks of the egg kingdom's leading authority on raising young eggs.

His gushing wife insists he's become almost as big a celebrity as King Crumpets. Humpty shakes his shell. "This isn't about me. Notoriety from a magazine only matters if it makes it possible for me to get more of my message out."

Before Humpty goes to bed, the kingdom's newspaper, The Egg Kingdom chronicle, calls and offers him a weekly column where he'll discuss the problems of young eggs.

Court's Scene Seven

Critic Crap

I'd grown up thinking I had to fight every critic. Wrong! I have to thank a strange woman with a pointed nose for teaching me one of my most valuable writing lessons.

I'd found my true calling writing young adult stories and worked at it day after day. I thought the Napoleon Prince adventure was my best work, but I couldn't get a publisher interested. Twenty letters with a red-stamped rejected at the top convinced me I needed something fresh to take me to the next level. The main character, Napoleon Prince, would stay the same. I'd take a darker approach mixing the Salem witch trials with an elite boarding school run by the descendants of the burned witches. It took about six months to write a three-hundred page Napoleon Prince Mystery. There were witches, secret societies and an ancient curse so deadly it gave me nightmares. I called Napoleon's new adventure *The Clan of the Seven Crows*.

Now came the hard part, I had to take the Seven Crows out to the world. My first encounter with running into a real critic came when I got invited to a group for experienced writers. I read and reread the Seven Crows, knew it was a riveting mystery and had visions of selling the movie rights for millions.

Six of us sat around a dining room table. There were two younger bearded guys, a gray haired woman wearing granny glasses, a middle-aged, bony lawyer, Gerald Pittman Esq. and a small, raspy voiced woman, Winfred Snow. She had a long, pointed nose and thick, bushy eyebrows and didn't hesitate to announce she'd just finished her new mystery.

We'd take turns reading for fifteen minutes, enough time to get through five pages. I'd be second from last. Our lawyer, Gerald Pittman Esq., his voice sounding like door hinges that needed to be oiled, went first. He had a courtroom drama about a grandmother serial killer with too much legal jargon. The pointed-nosed mystery writer, Winfred Snow, read second. Her story, which she read with detached confidence, took place in a nursing home where the residents kept mysteriously disappearing. It had great characters and smart dialogue.

My turn came and I didn't hold back. At the end of the reading the first two comments weren't enthusiastic. Only the lawyer liked the Salem Witches idea.

Then the mystery writer had her turn. She arched her eyebrows in a way that made it look like she had caterpillars crawling across her forehead, leaned over the table and locked her eyes on mine. Her high-pitched, screeching voice filled every corner of the room. "It's crap, nothing more than convoluted, confusing crap."

Winfred didn't get the meaning of constructive criticism. "Your main character's name sucks. The dialogue is wooden, this Prince kid isn't believable and the plot with all the demons and a secret clan doesn't make sense." I'll never forget how she summed up, "If this is for teenagers, then you should be accused of literary child abuse."

As if my nemesis had some dark power to sway everyone in the room, the others followed her lead and came up with a long list of faults. Gerald, the lawyer, pushed his eardrum rattling voice an octave higher. "After reflection I've have decided your main character, this Napoleon lad is quite immature and most decidedly uninteresting."

I turned my head away and thought I should surrender and tell them, if they'd stop their attacks, I'd quit writing. I'd opened myself up, dropped my defenses and protective attitude and shared what I thought was my best work. It felt like dad had come back from the grave in the body of my critic. As a grown man, I never remember coming so close to crying.

Winfred's and the other evaluations made the rest of the evening take on the feeling of a nightmare I couldn't get out of my head. At the end of the night, as everyone else walked out of the room, my first critic reached out, wrapped her fingers around my arm and pointed her nose in my direction. "Maybe you should try painting or playing the guitar."

At home, in the darkest mood I could remember, I considered deleting everything I'd written. I'd pull way back. There had to be something which didn't involve my self-esteem being ravaged.

The next morning, after a sleepless night, I went to the study and stared at a dark computer screen. The gruff inner advocate voice filled my head. "If it was easy everyone would be a writer. Look at it this way, maybe there were things your critic was right about."

What did I expect? Maybe there were things my critic had been right about. Suppose I'd fallen too much in love with the romance of writing, not the work and skill. Around noon the day after the writers group my inner critic and inner advocate had a major showdown.

The critic went first, "She nailed your weaknesses. The Napoleon Prince name is weird. What's more, the dialogue is wooden, too many of the characters are short on personality, and *The Clan of the Seven Crows* plot could be a lot clearer."

My advocate stormed in. "There's nothing she said you can't fix, besides you'd be a lousy painter and even worse as a guitar player. Look at this as a test to see if you really want to be a writer."

That afternoon I bought books on dialogue, character development and plotting. The next morning I started the first of three total revisions of *The Clan of the Seven Crows*, rewriting each chapter, changing the way I approached every part of my writing, and, to cover all my bases, I changed the main character's name to Jon Redmond.

One day I'd feel excited, like I could see the improvement and the next becoming a better writer seemed like an ordeal I wouldn't wish on my worst enemy.

I didn't go back to the writer's group for six months, until I felt the Seven Crows book had gotten out of the crap pile. This time seven writers attended, I'd read last. Before I could sit down the pointed-nosed Winfred Snow winked at me.

Why did I come back to this group? What a crazy, senseless idea, I should have known better. Maybe I turned into a masochist who took some kind of perverse pleasure in being humiliated.

Writer after writer read. I closed my eyes and tried to prepare myself for my real-life critic and the way she and the others would tear apart my story. I imagined Winfred stroking her caterpillar-like eyebrows and telling me, "You haven't gotten any better, the book is still crap. I said it before, you're no writer."

My turn came. Every other line my voice cracked. My antagonist took notes. Sweat ran down my forehead. I felt faint and pictured myself falling out of my chair. Somehow I got through the chapter and sat back waiting to be ravaged.

The comments from the other members of the group were positive. Everyone except my critic agreed I'd gotten much better. Not once did my eyes leave my glasses-wearing foe. The time finally arrived for Winfred to have at me.

Unlike the others, she didn't gush. Her comments were direct, but fair and helpful. She picked up some plot inconsistencies and suggested I delete a minor character, which made sense. I felt like one of those inmates whose execution is stayed right before they throw the switch. To make sure I got everything right, I forced myself to ask her a couple of questions.

On the way out she remained by the door and waited for me. When I went by she looked up and spoke just above a whisper. "I can tell how much blood and sweat you put into what you read. Congratulations, now you're a writer."

Winfred Snow had been harsh, but from her view fair. She gave me a way to make a big improvement in my writing. It's not easy to admit, but it's important to listen to critics.

Thanks to Winfred I'm a better writer and a lot closer to being published. It's not an easy road and I've been tested over and over. The trick for me is to listen to every bit of feedback and come up with stories incorporating the strong points in two opposing views.

STITCHING – <u>Connecting Scenes Seven and Eight</u>

I took my work out to the world, went public and got a mix of fans who helped me push forward and faultfinders who thought I was only fit to work at a burger stand. My return to the writers group and getting past Winfred gave me new confidence.

Along the way Sylvia and I studied Jungian psychology, courses on the Self, individuation, and my favorite, active imagination. I learned to enhance my writing by working with my unconscious and not being afraid of memories I'd repressed.

An out of the blue challenge took my writing in a surprising new direction—you wouldn't be reading this book if it hadn't. All those revisions of my first books, studying every imaginable writing element, working with active imagination and connecting with my unconscious paid off in a surprising way.

Sylvia's Scene Seven

Midnight Samurai

The bell on my antique French clock sounded midnight. I sat in my chair wide awake staring at a painting of a Japanese *Samurai*. The orange background and gray and gold robes with long hair blowing in the breeze; he looked so alive, intense and unafraid. I wanted to be him. He wouldn't have trouble stating publicly what he could bring to the world and wouldn't think twice about taking on all challengers.

Tomorrow I'd be with a group of friends I've invited to my home. I wanted the Samurai to step out of the painting and help me find my courage.

There'd be Alexandra, an elegantly-dressed brilliant architect, Stella, a no-nonsense businesswoman who owns a local flower shop, Cassie, a lively stay at home mom with two kids ready for college and Zoe, a studious high school science teacher.

They'll be the first ones I show my Cycle Journey. It describes the eight-stage journey which moves beyond a Dark Night. The colorful two-page flyer on my desk that Court and I have worked on for a month summarizes the work I've done. It looks imposing, like it came out of a university think tank. A picture of the cycle is on the front—it seems so real, like it could be a book cover. In a few hours I'll make my first public proclamation of my Cycle Journey Concept.

My hands are shaking. There's a tightening knot in my stomach. Like a little girl getting ready for her first day of school, my imagination is going wild. Over and over my inner critic cautions me, "Sylvia, you're no professor. Suppose they question your ideas and you can't come up with answers? Even worse they might call your cycle ridiculous and laugh at you."

My faultfinder has lots of practice holding me back. For years the ever-present fear I can't handle disapproval stopped me from sharing my ideas.

Before I turned in I meditated, asked my inner advocate to come forward. The wise, confident voice helped me see I needed a deepened perspective. "Proclaim what you care deeply about. The cycle can help people disillusioned with their life and crippled by their own inner critic. They need your strength."

I could choose to make today an opportunity, one where like the Samurai warrior in the painting, I would push fearlessly forward and state publically for the first time a life-changing message which saved me and could help so many people.

The next morning, after five hours sleep I and my four guests seated ourselves around my living room, Alexandra on my left and Zoe on my right and Stella and Cassie across from me. I took a deep breath and started by sharing my fear about presenting the cycle. Everyone stayed quiet. I held up the two-page brochure and told the story of how it came into being. A few minutes into the presentation my excitement took over.

The cycle got an involved response. Stella, the flower store owner, told me, "Sylvia, after my mother died I went through a Dark Night and felt abandoned and lost. Your transformational journey makes so much sense. Tell us more about the stages."

I took about fifteen minutes to review the stages. When I finished Alexandra, Cassie and Zoe couldn't wait to tell me which stage they'd decided they were in.

We finished and Cassie, the stay at home mom, came up and took my hand. I could see tears. "Sylvia, I don't want to imagine myself going through your cycle. After all I've been through in the last couple of years with the kids, there is no way I can look any closer at my life. It would bring up too many painful memories."

I told her I understood and gave her a hug.

Zoe, the science teacher, had a skeptical look. "Sylvia you're in real estate not psychology and this cycle business isn't verifiable science. I see problems, like suppose the person going through the Dark Night is an emotional wreck and isn't focused enough to even figure out where they are in your cycle. You're not qualified to give advice."

I nodded. "The Humpty Dumpty Principle is meant for a general audience, for individuals who've experienced a Dark Night and challenging times. It's based on Court's and my experiences. We want to give people a structure for what seems like a chaotic time and provide strategies to help make sense out of what happened."

Zoe shook her head. "You're not answering my question about professional help."

"Professional help is important. I see the Cycle Journey as a way for people to realize they may need a professional view and reach out for guidance. I'm a living example of someone who had a Dark Night and had the good sense to know I needed outside help."

Alexandra, the architect, waited until I'd finished with Zoe. She hugged me. "Your Cycle Journey is wonderful. I can't wait until you have it in a booklet or even better a book. After your talk about the wandering stage, I understand what happened when Ron and I broke up. You helped me see I've been drifting and it's time to move on."

As Alexandra walked toward the front door, I had what seemed like an out-of-body experience. I could see myself teaching the cycle. For the first time realized I had an idea I could take out to the world. In my imagination I stood in front of a large audience and told them, "Today we'll talk about a very special journey, one beginning with a great fall that brings a Dark Night." Everyone clapped wildly.

Over the years I'd passed up many opportunities to talk about how people go through their own Self-discovery. Sharing the Cycle Journey, something I cared about so much, had been a pivotal moment. I'd helped myself move past my fear of sharing my ideas and I felt courageous, almost as if the *Samurai* had granted my wish and transferred his fearless attitude to me.

What I learned out of proclaiming to my friends is my only limitations had been self-imposed. There are countless women and men struggling to escape Dark Nights. I had a question for my inner wisdom. If I set my imagination free, how far could I take my Dark Night and Cycle Journey ideas?

The answer came instantly, almost as if my Self had been waiting for me to ask. "You can write a book." Write a book, again and again the words ran through my mind—why not?

STITCHING - <u>Connecting</u> <u>Scenes Seven and Eight:</u>

I'd lived through Dark Nights, experienced each stage of the journey, changed my life view and stopped my destructive patterns. For a couple of weeks I considered the pluses and minuses of putting my ideas on paper. A book on my Cycle Journey would be a next growth step. Once I finished I could teach the process, which would be another dream come true.

My book writing adventure turned out to be more than I bargained for. After months of writing and revising, I hit a wall and almost gave up. The idea to ask Court to work with me came with such clarity it shocked me. Why hadn't I thought of it before? One problem, I had to convince him it was a great idea.

Tell * Journal * Write

Scene Seven

Our coaching advice is to write about how you'll use your imagination to take your new destiny into the world. We're cheerleaders who want to build your confidence that, in spite of the doubters, you can do it.

Your scene seven displays a realization you have the skills and have done the preparation necessary to proclaim quest results to family, friends, and co-workers, and anyone interested in your newly claimed destiny.

Your scene needs to show everyone you're serious about making a formal declaration of your quest results. Describe how you'll declare publicly and insistently in speech, writing or actions you've moved beyond your Dark Night and embraced an authentic destiny.

Court's opening **core sentence** states his change of viewpoint. "It amazing how often the truth is the opposite of what you've thought for years. I'd grown up thinking I had to fight every critic. Wrong! I have to thank a strange woman with a pointed nose for teaching me one of my most valuable writing lessons."

Sylvia's **core sentence** presents the challenge of her initial proclaiming. "Tomorrow I'd be with a group of friends I've invited to my home. I wanted the Samurai to step out of the painting and help me find my courage."

Scene seven is the last step before transforming. Show a commitment deep enough to withstand outer critics and exciting enough to thrill outer advocates. Your scene resolves around how you plan to take your quest results public. There's no turning back and you'll write about how your proclaiming commitment is absolute. You're ready to trumpet the success of your quest adventure.

Your attitude reflects the mix of emotions in the scene. You might be anxious, a little on edge and perhaps a little afraid. The proclaiming scene needs tension. You'll try to anticipate the different reactions to quest results. Who will and won't accept your new destiny. Tell about how you've created an atmosphere where you can talk about the full range of your emotional makeup.

The cycle stages have drawn out chaotic emotions. You realize proclaiming, facing the outside world and telling others about your new destiny could meet with rejection. **That expectation of opposition creates fear and tension and often brings on new conflicts.**

Use dialogue or descriptions to reflect your changing emotions. Pick words and phrases showing tension, conflict, and fear. Short, emotionally charged words like chaos, anger, excitement, danger, panic, enthusiasm, eagerness, and anticipation convey intensity. Similes such as my hands shook like I'd seen a ghost or I felt like a string pulled so tight it would snap any moment bring the mix to life.

Bring the **creativity and imagination of your sixth sense** into proclaiming. What are different ways to tell the world about your quest? Whether it's a social media presentation, quest photos or even this scene can make proclaiming more exciting.

Focus on how you use your inner critic and advocate to evaluate proclaiming and answer outer critics or realistically assess what outer advocates are telling you. When you get feedback, especially critical feedback, write it into your scene. Revise your scene so that you can strengthen your advocate's answers.

There is a choice in how you employ **setting and props**. Location or surroundings can support or conflict with the tone and word choice.

For example, among other possible associations, an office might generate a sterile or inviting mood and a hotel lobby could be chaotic or calming. Depending on its importance in the scene, it can be a detailed description or it can provide minimal details. A prop like a social media presentation or a short paper with your main points adds to your proclaiming. Be careful these supports don't take away the intimate or spontaneous feeling.

The setting Sylvia uses in her scene seven is her own home. She needs to feel safe to take the risk of presenting her Cycle Journey. Notice she uses a prop, a brochure, to give herself a focal point for her presentation to her friends. In Court's proclaiming scene, he goes public with his writing and faces a difficult critic. It's a wakeup call for him.

He has to regroup to get past withering criticism. In your scene don't be afraid to show fear and discouragement and how you had to reach acceptance at a new level before you could face a strong critic.

Most proclaimers face a mix of criticism and praise. A scene that helps you deal with the variety of responses is a necessary part of any move toward transformation.

Words to improve your proclaiming scene are:

Announce	Go Public	Society
Declare	External	Community
Broadcast	A Jury	Verdict
State Publically	Opening	Judges
Make Known	Sharing	World At Large

The deepened insights and expanded awareness you add focus on new possibilities. Like Court you can get past a harsh critic or like Sylvia a presentation could lead to a book. Open yourself to the new possibilities that create transformation. Be specific about how the feedback you've gotten in proclaiming has changed your Self-image and given you the assurance you need to see there is a new you, a person who is fundamentally changed.

EIGHT

The Purple Stage, Transform

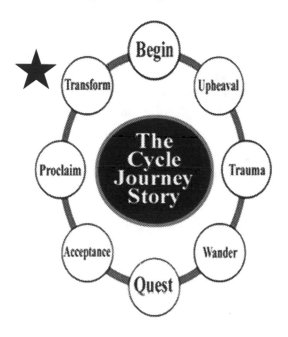

A Union of Inner and Outer Wisdom Brings Balance

"We all have moments in life when we know we are touched
by a force that is larger than ourselves, something very real
that transcends our experience of the ordinary world."
~Lionel Corbett, Jungian Analyst

An Introduction To Stage Eight

This is it. You're at the end of the Cycle Journey and still transforming seems like a magic trick. The eighth stage teaches belief in the possibility of change which is a necessary requirement for transformation.

Professor Henry Higgins from My Fair Lady, Apple's Steve Jobs and civil rights pioneer Rosa Parks make up the uncommon trio of transformational poster people. With transformation being its own Deeper Insight, the stage moves toward the conclusion of Humpty's and our stories. Our renowned egg has realized that in his transformation there is the power to change the entire egg kingdom. Our story of how we wrote this book is an illustration of transformation enriching a relationship by giving it a new direction and purpose.

The Stage Eight Tell * Journal * Write coaching centers on the package of writing skills necessary to sum up your journey.

The Essentials

Change, especially in a Cycle Journey, has its seeds in youth and reveals its true form in an upheaval. In the quest you undertook the search for a new destiny. **As the end of the journey approaches, you see the Dark Night you thought robbed you of meaning actually brought the gift of life-changing purpose.**

You've needed willpower and insight to move from one stage to the next. Your self-confidence reached a new high when you overcame perils which threatened to delay or derail the journey. Through seven stages, despite the dangers and risks, you've used inner wisdom to guide you to the stage where transformation is possible.

The Cycle's purple stage is an evolution away from an outer-directed life defined by others and the culture to an inner-directed life where there is an internal understanding of the lessons learned during the journey.

There is now a bridge between the unconscious and the conscious and many once repressed memories are available to you. The **active imagination** connection you've used for your scenes opened up a creative flow which led to a new sense of individuation. **Wholeness and balance that lead you to an appreciation of who you are and who you were meant to be are part of your life.**

For change to take hold you need a transformation experience. Something, a visible symbol, test, extreme challenge or ordeal is needed before you can know if the change is real and deep. It could be a marathon, or completing a nearly impossible work project. You might climb a mountain or put in the day and night work necessary to bring a new product to market.

However, just the challenge isn't enough. You need to open to new ideas, try different approaches, explore creative avenues or let your imagination run free.

Transformation has a last requirement, belief. You must have realized a compelling, unbreakable conviction you have changed for good. There is an inner understanding that the acceptance and proclaiming stages have prepared you to acknowledge your new destiny without reservation, equivocation, or conditions.

In My Fair Lady, Professor Henry Higgins sets out to transform Cockney flower girl Eliza Doolittle into a lady. The film is based on George Bernard Shaw's play Pygmalion, taken from Ovid's poem about a sculptor who falls in love with a statue he'd created and what happens when the goddess Aphrodite grants his wish to make the statue come alive.

In the film and play Higgins is only concerned with Eliza's exterior change. What he doesn't comprehend until Eliza leaves him is his demand for perfection created a transformation experience. Eliza has gained an unshakable belief she has changed on the inside. She has, like Pygmalion's statue, fully come to life.

Transformation, a change into a new and different person, an evolved Self, is easiest to see on the outside. Deeper growth takes place internally. Your experience changes you, like it did Eliza, into a person with expanded inner awareness and new, deeper insights.

The eighth stage of the journey is about ongoing external and internal change. Opposing energies are brought into balance and there is a new understanding of being guided by an authentic destiny. This union creates a sense of resolution and a feeling you're at the end of a long and challenging journey symbolized by purple being the last color in a rainbow.

Walter Isaacson's *Steve Jobs* biography takes shape in 1985 when at age thirty Jobs founded Apple Computer. The upheaval happened when John Scully forced Jobs out of the company he founded. Steve Jobs is an extraordinary figure, a different kind of transformation poster boy. Imagine a new-age truth seeker who's both charming and an arrogant control freak and has an overlay of expanded awareness. His genius sense of design, shaped by world-class creativity and combined with an insistence on product perfection made him a singular leader.

Jobs left his own company, started NeXT computer, and bought majority control in the highly successful Pixar Animation. At age forty, in 1997 when Apple bought NeXT, Jobs came back to his company with two transformation experiences and a deep belief he could take his company back and run it successfully. The previous year Apple lost 1.04 billion dollars. Jobs bought it back to profitability in the first quarter after he returned.

What's most interesting about the adopted Jobs, who had a pattern of relying on and feeling betrayed by older men he saw as father figures, is his experiences matured and transformed him, but didn't change his basic difficult and uncompromising nature. He understood his gift and the responsibility that came with it. Over time he'd learned how to use his abrasive personality to create a string of products of unrivaled brilliance.

Rosa Parks, the African-American civil rights activist, went through a contrasting transformation. On December 1st, 1955, in Montgomery, Alabama, Parks refused to follow the bus driver's command she give her seat in the colored section to a white person and was arrested.

In her autobiography, *My Story*, she tells how her resistance grew out of her childhood experience where buses took white students to their school, while black students had to walk to theirs.

She states her moment of truth, her own conversion experience in *My Story* when she writes, "People always said I was tired, but that isn't true ………….. No, the only tired I was, was tired of giving in." Her quote compellingly expresses a belief which allowed her to stand up to centuries old racial inequalities.

Nowhere is a transformation's sense of balance more evident than in two books about India's Mahatma Gandhi, William L. Shiner's *Gandhi, A Memoir,* and *Great Men in History, Gandhi* by Steven Knott. Raised in a Hindu merchant cast family, Gandhi's early life, Indian stories and religious training, gave him the strong sense of truth and love he carried through his life. His experiences under British rule in South Africa and India allowed him to see a new non-violent way to put his heritage to work. Two of his quotes show the balance and wholeness of a transformation.

**"Happiness is when what you think, what you
say and what you do are in harmony."**

This quote says you can bring the inner critic and advocate together and choose a middle road. The next Gandhi lines capture the essence of the evolution that takes place in transformation.

"Keep your thoughts positive because your thoughts become your words. Keep your words positive because your words become your behavior. Keep your behavior positive because your behavior becomes your habits. Keep your habits positive because your habits become your values. Keep your values positive because your values become your destiny."

Steve Jobs time after he left Apple, Rosa Parks' memories of walking to school while white students rode on buses, and Gandhi's early identification with Indian cultural and religious traditions built the foundation for their dramatic changes. Those experiences in the natural flow of their lives moved them toward forming the strong individualized personalities they needed to claim their important destinies and allowed them to carry their experiences through the rest of their lives. Notice age and the different situations they faced put no limitations on Jobs, Parks and Gandhi's ability to transform.

Lionel Corbett has a simple answer for living in the natural flow of life. "It does not matter whether we are swept away by music or gardening, dancing or surfing. Anything that takes us out of the ego into a state of flow and out of ordinary time is a spiritual pursuit..... Everyday life can become an expression of spirituality."

After The Transformation:

The ordinary world, people, places and things, haven't changed, it's you who has a new, deeper way to understand what transpires in your life. For a while the world feels foreign and it's often difficult to interact with those who can't grasp your inner transformation. The quote, "It's never too late to be what you might have been." by novelist Mary Ann Evans writing as George Eliot, is an ideal way to look at your new life path.

The end of one journey is often the beginning of another. Your conscious awareness has expanded and you have insights which give you a new view of the world. It's possible another journey awaits and another level of growth is there for the asking.

The phrase the never ending journey might refer to the true potential the Cycle Journey holds. If you have the courage and fortitude to embrace its full potential it's entirely possible transforming has no defined end or destination.

The Stories For Stage Eight

The King
**"Beloved wife my great fall may have been
the best thing that ever happened."**

Court and Sylvia's Scene Eight:

Collaboration

From our final scene: Webster say "to transform implies a major changes in form, substance, nature, or function." It surprises us every day how much our natures and the way we function in the world have altered. In a very real and concrete way finishing the Humpty Dumpty Principle taught us an essential truth. Change comes with a test. All the obstacles and roadblocks, every dead end where you toss out the last ten pages you've written is part of your change experience. If you don't push yourself beyond your ordinary limits, if you don't open up to new ideas, if you don't allow for deeper beliefs then you haven't had a true conversion.

Your Cycle Journey Story:
Scene Eight - Transformation

Humpty's Story Continues:
Chapter Eight: The King

"Face facts, there's not enough time in the day." Humpty tells his wife. "Today is the beginning of our annual summer camp out and the young eggs will be coming in from all over the kingdom. It'll bring back memories of my young counselor days."

His wife's smile is full of admiration as she kisses his shell right on one of its biggest cracks. "Husband dear, you're the ideal example of a good egg. I've heard at a meeting of the king's council they talked of nominating you for egg of the year."

Humpty beams and tells her, "Beloved wife my great fall may have been the best thing that ever happened. The day I climbed up on the wall and the dark days after the terrible tumble seems so distant. I've never been happier than I am this very minute. My life has turned sunny side up. I'm making a real difference in the kingdom by helping the egglets."

Later in the day Humpty arrives at the campground the egg community built on the edge of the hatchery. Duck eggs and smaller brown and spotted quail eggs are in the middle of a spirited egg roll. Goose eggs and ostrich eggs are tossing a laughing gull egg back and forth. There's a group of brown pheasant eggs painting purple lines around their shells. A troupe of damaged shell egglets Humpty recruited to the camp is happily singing the old classic, *Roll On, Roll On, You Magnificent Sphere.*

The different egglets are getting along wonderfully. Best of all none of the campers are ridiculing the youngsters marked by cracks and missing pieces.

Humpty has banned judgmental troublemakers, like the League for the Suppression of Unsightly Eggs, from the camp. To enrich the camper's cultural knowledge, he's invited speakers, including a famous sculptor, Augustus Von Yokestus, and Conrad Shellburn, the composer who wrote the hit opera, The Marriage of Eggero. Humpty tells visitors the camp is about teaching young egglets the rich culture of the egg kingdom and to be tolerant and inclusive.

The next day, just before lunch, there is the sound of trumpets coming from the direction of the castle. Seconds later the king's ministers on their high prancing stallions lead the gleaming royal coach into the campground. The campers gather around as old King Claudius Crumpets the Extra-Large, his golden crown gleaming in the sun and his diamond-studded shell inspiring awe, steps out of the coach.

The old king, leaning on a cane decorated with rubies and diamonds, is easily four times the size of the largest ostrich egg and said to be able to trace his lineage back to the legendary elephant bird eggs from the dinosaur age.

King Crumpets clears his throat as his Prime Minister hands him a large, shiny, star-shaped medal on a golden chain. The king holds up the medal so the campers can see it, and tells Humpty, "Mr. Dumpty, my ministers have informed me you've dedicated your life to helping the kingdom's young eggs. First rate, all my subjects can learn from your example. It is my great, great pleasure to honor you as the kingdom's Egg Extraordinary, and personally present you with the *Bon Oeuf* medal, the highest accolade I can bestow upon any subject."

The moment the king's coach departs Humpty leaves the campground. He wants to return home and tell his wife and the egglets about the award.

The next morning, still back at his carton, he awakes before dawn. He can barely believe all that's happened since his great fall. He's found his true calling, the place in the world he was always meant to be. It's as if he's been reborn. He dresses in his camp leader shorts and boots, slips his whistle around his shell and heads outside, intent on getting back to the camp as quickly as possible.

An overpowering idea emerges from his yoke. In the dim early morning light Humpty makes his way to the back of the carton and grabs the ladder. With the ladder swaying from side to side, he hurries down the road and soon arrives at the wall. The first rays of sunlight are peeking through the clouds at the moment he lays the ladder against the wall's red bricks, climbs to the top, looks out and utters a startled cry.

The forest is no longer dark. The gray mist has lifted. Before him a field of bright yellow daffodils, as if they are waving, sway in the morning breeze. Behind the flowers he sees the true forest, a limitless expanse of gloriously green pines and darker green yews.

He climbs on the wall's ledge and sits. His feet dangle down. Astonished, he stares at more beauty than he ever imagined possible.

"Quite something isn't it egg, the dark forest being gone I mean." Down at the bottom of the wall Reynard is staring up at him.

The fox shakes its head. "Not exactly sure what happened. The makeover started yesterday morning. At first only a few rays of light burned through the mist. By evening the darkness disappeared. It's unexplainable, as if the darkness decided it no longer had a place in the forest. On the other hand it's quite lovely and there's so much to see." Reynard raises a paw and waves before he runs and jumps across the field of daffodils and disappears in the pines.

Moments later Basil the witch's crow lands on the ledge beside Humpty and looks up. "Egg, the witch and creatures in the dark forest underestimated your power. The ghosts and demons have left the forest. Last I saw of her the witch tied her kettle to her broom and flew off to look for where the darkness is hiding. I've decided to stay. It's so beautiful I can't leave."

Humpty stares at the sun-drenched woods and has a thought so profound it makes his yoke bubble. *Could it be my transformation turned the tide? The kingdom-wide interest in the young eggs may have altered the nature of the entire egg kingdom. It's like a transformation where the darkness no longer has a place to reside.*

Before he climbs down, Humpty runs his hands over his shell, smiles and decides his idea about the power of change isn't far-fetched. He leaves the ladder at the wall. In the future there could come a time when the dark mist returns and another egg might need to learn the lesson of the great fall and the benefits of a journey of personal change.

Court and Sylvia's Scene Eight

Collaboration

Scene eight is not about one specific incident or being at a single stage in our Cycle Journeys. We used this scene to write about what completing the Humpty Dumpty Principle meant to us and how writing it brought profound change to our world.

Over the past year Sylvia and I had countless discussions on how to explain the Cycle Journey. There were raised voices. Again and again we've been stunned by our lack of an ability to see the obvious, like the importance of a contemplative attitude in acceptance or how the tension of opposites defines the true role of the inner critic and inner advocate. When it came to adding Deeper Insights, like Jung's shadow concept or the role active imagination plays in moving through the cycle, our intuitions had growth spurts. The structure of the book, and explaining **The Tell * Journal * Write Concept** challenged our creativity and imaginations. Many of our morning conferences ended up taking a good part of the day and our late night discussions left us sleep deprived. Those are only a few symptoms of the deep personal change this book brought to us.

The struggle to finish the Humpty Dumpty Principle taught us an essential truth, change comes with a test. All the obstacles and roadblocks, every dead end where you toss out the last ten pages is part of your change experience. If you don't push yourself beyond ordinary limits, if you don't open up to new ideas, if you don't allow for deeper beliefs then you haven't had a true conversion.

Along the way we had an opportunity to take our relationship to a new level. In the end, near completion, we understood the book itself had altered the way we interacted with the world. Over the year we worked together our belief in the reality of the Cycle Journey Story pushed us past hurdle after hurdle.

Sylvia told me the idea we'd collaborate on the Humpty Dumpty Principle came to her late at night when she'd been staring at her laptop. She'd spent every free minute working on what she thought would be a small booklet on her Cycle Journey Concept.

Her sliding house, the horrible ski accident, the time with her therapist, her schooling and presenting her cycle to her friends left her feeling she'd been called to write about the Cycle Journey. The further she got into the stages, the more the book turned into a challenge, one she didn't know if she could complete.

She decided to use a noteworthy advantage, she lived with a writer. Sylvia came up to my desk, laid two bracelets we'd bought a few weeks earlier in front of me and pointed to the write your own way inscriptions. After a dramatic pause she looked into my eyes and told me, "I'm having trouble writing my own way. Maybe it's time to see if we can write our own way."

Sylvia waited for me to catch up. "To make my little book work I'm going to need your writing expertise. Don't worry, it's only supposed to be a booklet I'll give to my friends."

On our way to bed Sylvia had a last thought. "Yesterday I had this vision of Saint John in his prison cell writing his Dark Night of the Soul poem. Imagine how he'd feel if he knew his ideas reached across the centuries and how his willingness to suffer for his beliefs made the world a better place for so many people. Think over what I told you and we'll talk tomorrow."

The next morning over coffee I told her my biggest concern. "What happens when we butt heads?"

"Are you saying you don't think we can work together? What a scary lack of confidence." Sylvia laughed. "Maybe you're worried you can't handle something this serious."

Over the weekend for the first time I had a chance to read what she'd written. How people could change after a Dark Night had a fascinating appeal. One paragraph caught my attention. "Do you remember the Mother Goose nursery rhyme Humpty Dumpty and the line about his great fall? After a Dark Night people picture themselves having had a great fall and broken into pieces with no idea of how they can put themselves together again."

A light went on. What about using creative non-fiction techniques to make the Cycle Journey come alive? Maybe I had more of a connection to Sylvia's project than I thought. Suppose Humpty told the story of his own great fall. It would be an allegory that exposed readers to a view of the Dark Night and the Cycle Journey in a clear every person or in this case, an every egg format they could grasp.

That evening I wrote the tale of how Humpty moved past his great fall. It would serve as a less threatening and gloomy way to show how the Cycle Journey operated.

The next day the moment Sylvia walked through the door I pointed to a chair and blurted out everything. "Humpty Dumpy should serve as a symbol for the people who have a Dark Night and begin a Cycle Journey. We need a statement or principle for his journey. We could call the book the *Humpty Dumpty Story* or maybe *The Humpty Dumpty Principle*. We'll frame your cycle as what happened to Humpty after his great fall. The principle could be "The Great Fall brings a Dark Night. Don't wait for all the king's horses and all the king's men. You can put yourself together again."

Sylvia's smiled. "I love it and know we can make it work."

The way the book came together over the next year is a lesson in how change has its own agenda. It evolved from a thirty page booklet to an almost three-hundred page book. There were bumps and more than once we felt we'd taken on more than we could handle.

Our stories became a key turning point. They needed to be more than a descriptive retelling of our journeys. We had to dig deeper. This book would have to look into our inner worlds. It would tell the feelings and emotions attached to our journeys. We'd use the eight stages of cycle as a structure for our stories, with each stage being a story scene.

The closer we came to finishing The Humpty Dumpty Principle, the more we realized we could bring an important message to the world. We'd developed an approach loaded with fresh insights on the meaning of a Dark Night. For the first time we understood an old alchemist's saying, "The goal is the art." The saying showed us transforming, true change, is a test of sincerity and commitment.

More than the individual changes, working together on The Humpty Dumpty Principle taught us the power of two people combining their skills. We wrote a book neither of us could have done alone. Our combined talents overcame limitations and magnified strengths. We shared a consuming passion and a way to put the last pieces of our own Dark Nights to rest.

This book taught us when you least expect it another path opens up and gives you the chance to stop caring about the cracks in your own shell and move on to the things which really count.

A Stitching Postscript <u>Connecting Scene Eight to the Rest of Life</u>

We are ready to introduce the Principle to the world. It's scary and at the same time the possibilities are thrilling. Every day we see ways to give people deeper insights into the meaning of their lives by telling, journaling, and writing their own stories. We realize how the cycle can give our readers a fresh way to look at challenging times in their lives. Sometimes we imagine Humpty Dumpty on the wall just before his fall and think he'd be very happy if he knew what his terrible tumble set into motion.

Court's Conclusion

Most of my life seemed chaotic and random. After writing my story, I see a structure and patterns unfolding. Sometimes it feels otherworldly, like someone else had such a difficult father and all those nonsensical jobs. At the same time I know I didn't get to where I am by accident.

I've tied my tumultuous childhood and youth to my adult life and understand how much of an influence my beginning had on me. I wanted stability and predictability, but didn't realize the overpowering need I have to make creativity and imagination a central part of my life.

My divorce became an earthquake-like shock, the upheaval that shook my world to its core. I turned into a rootless wanderer with few responsibilities or close connections. Through the quest, acceptance, and proclaiming stages, I've struggled to come to terms with an authentic destiny I now see had always waited for me. In the end transforming happened without me realizing it. My likes and dislikes have been remixed more than I ever expected. It seems like hardly a day goes by without me surprising myself.

A little over a year ago, when I started my scenes I thought I'd be embarrassed to tell the story, warts and all, of my strange adventures. In writing this conclusion, what astounds me is how much this single book has changed my view of life.

At each stage of the journey, from Moline, Illinois and a chaotic childhood to Southern California and a checkered job history, and from Santa Barbara and the search for my own unique voice to writing the Humpty Dumpty Principle, I've moved toward a transformation that brought me wholeness and a new life path.

The intense satisfaction I've experienced in writing my Cycle Journey Story has reshaped me at the deepest level. The best way I can describe it is I feel like I've reclaimed my life and can understand its goal and purpose.

Court Johnson

Sylvia's Conclusion

The Cycle Journey became an odyssey, a series of experiences which gave me knowledge and understanding about the course my life has followed. Over many months I've examined and re-examined significant parts of my journey, got a new view of how they affected me, and realized I could let outdated parts of my history go.

Letting go of old ideas, deeply hurt feelings, and dark fearful places are growth steps I've worked to enact. Learning to forgive myself and others for the betrayals, disappointments, and mistakes has replaced an old way of thinking and being, and brought a new sense of peace and joy to my life. To find true love I needed to love myself just as I am and not how I should be. As I grow and become more kind and loving, I experience more kindness and love from others. I've realized the source of love comes from inside, spreads into the world and returns in its own way and time.

Writing my story hasn't been easy. There have been constant revisions and a never-ending challenge to look deeper. The day I finished my Cycle Journey Story I looked back and saw the scenes produced a shift within me. I'm finally free to be who I am and who I was meant to be. What's remarkable is I've changed from living an outer-directed life and conforming to what others and the world expects of me, to the peaceful freedom of an inner-directed life based on inner wisdom from my true and authentic Self.

It's a challenge to describe this change because it's so much more than an intellectual exercise. The Cycle Journey and telling my story brought about a visceral, deep feeling of change, as if I'd connected with an undiscovered part of myself.

I believe this powerful sense of Self is what transforming is about. This fresh viewpoint with its flow of insights and awareness astounds me by how it has changed the way I see the world. Today it's so much easier to see the whole picture instead of the pieces and look for possibilities instead of limitations. I realize this is only a beginning of another part of my life which until now I didn't know existed.

Sylvia Stallings

Tell * Journal * Write

Scene Eight

We've given you the viewpoint of a coach, teacher, motivator, guide, and cheerleader. Those perspectives unite in transformation where you'll bring together what you learned in the other seven stages. At this final phase of your Cycle Journey you've embraced a new approach to challenges which allows you to begin again.

Transformation is the most conceptual of the stages. It has its own underlying words to convey the different aspects of how your Cycle Journey influenced you.

- Transformation is about **deep change**, becoming different. There's the old you, the version which existed before you began your Cycle Journey, and there is the improved you, the result of a personal change. Write about what's different.
- Transformation is an internal **makeover**. Inside you feel more alive. Fresh ideas are coming into your mind. Put the new thoughts into your last scene.
- Transformation is **alteration**. What's changed? Are you more patient, curious, or forceful? In your scene be specific about the different ways you interact in the world.
- Transformation can be a **metamorphosis**, a profound, inner change. Where's the difference? Is it in friends, activities or new knowledge or in your ability to be introspective?
- Transformation is part **conversion**, a decisive shift of viewpoint. How has your outlook been altered? Give examples of the ways you see the world differently.
- Transformation feels like a **transfiguration**, a spiritual change. Do you sense you have a deepened outlook?
- Transformation is the true **turning point** where there is an evolution of awareness and an intensifying of insights. What are examples of new awareness?

The eighth stage requires the best word choice. It needs a sense you understand what the Cycle Journey is all about and a realization the eight stages have brought about compelling and lasting change. For Humpty the darkness left the forest. Court and Sylvia completed the Humpty Dumpty Principle and realized its possibilities gave new meaning and purpose to their twenty-two year relationship.

Tell * Journal * Write a scene that has your unconscious open up to non-literal, figurative language which paints mental pictures of your transformation. This approach uses imagery to open the mind's eye and view the deep changes you've made.

Pick out a transformational change **symbol**. The Humpty Dumpty Principle, the book itself, is a symbol for Court and Sylvia. They chart their personal changes by their struggles with different parts of the book.

One final point, the eighth stage **stitching postscript** is a speculative look at your future. Where will the Cycle Journey take you? What are the possibilities that spring from long-lasting change? Where will you be in another year, in five years, or in another decade? What are the long-range changes the Cycle Journey brought to your life?

When your scenes are complete, write a **conclusion** which summarizes where the Cycle Journey led you. Show the changes between when you began the story and when you wrote the final scene.

You've completed the journey through eight stages. Think about the power that's been placed in your hands. A great fall that brought a Dark Night became a unique opportunity to change course. You now have the skills necessary to reweave the fabric of your life. To begin all you have to do is write the first word in the first scene of your Cycle Journey Story.

<u>Background</u>

Six Steps
For Assembling Your Cycle Journey Story

Looking Back At
Your Cycle Journey Story
Featuring

The Tell * Journal * Write Concept

Cycle Journey Pillars
C. G. Jung
Saint John of the Cross

A Review of Literature
Seventeen Books That Support the Cycle Journey

Six Steps For Assembling Your Cycle Journey Story

1. Put all your scenes in one book or file.
2. Write a list of scenes. They have become the chapters in your story
3. Un-bold the stitching and take out the title line so it becomes the last paragraph or paragraphs in each scene and connects to the next scene. If necessary, to make the transition smooth, add more detail to what is now the last scene paragraph.
4. Add your conclusion.
5. Use a binder with a plastic cover to hold your story. Insert a cover page with the title The Cycle Journey Story and add your name.
6. Pat yourself on the back. You've done it, written a full account of a journey which is uniquely yours.

Looking Back At Your Cycle Journey Story

The Tell * Journal * Write Concept

To start to tell your Cycle Journey Story, you became a storyteller, a narrator who verbalized his or her story. You picked a family member or a close friend and told them one of your scenes, and you made the scene come alive by using voices and hand gestures. Your listener felt the energy and spontaneity behind the scene. Each time you told your story your unconscious participated more actively. When there was no one to listen to your scene, you became your own audience by talking to a mirror.

The journal you kept was filled with messages from your creativity, imagination and intuition. The random ideas that came into your mind or sudden thoughts that burst into your consciousness became part of the journal. With a free-flow journal you found improved access to imagination-based insights that brought necessary feelings and emotions into your story.

What surprised you most is telling your story and keeping a journal of random thoughts made it seem almost natural to write a scene. You realized using **The Tell * Journal * Write Concept** meant you had already shaped the narrative and you understood the logic behind your story.

Telling, journaling and writing became the interactive components of building your scenes. You've told the story and wrote based on what you've heard then added creative unconscious input from your journal. You've dramatically improved your Cycle Journey Story when you used the full power of **The Tell * Journal * Write Concept**.

Evaluating The Personal Odyssey in Your Story:

Here are some standards for you to use to see if your scenes have the focus they need.

- You've kept the focal point of each scene on you and your feelings and emotions.
- Upheaval blame hasn't been assigned to others.
- You didn't try to get even or make someone else feel bad over the way they treated you. Finger pointing and accusations have been left out of your scenes.

By deepening your understanding and expanding your Self-knowledge you have learned and grown from your Dark Night.

Different Perspectives On The Uses Of Your Story:

- You've completed your story, a mini-memoir, but have decided to keep it for your eyes only. You believe this retelling of chaotic times is a story only you can fully comprehend.
- You plan to share your story. You want friends, family or someone close to hear or read your story.
- You've developed your story with the goal of publishing it.

There will be scenes where you've avoided a direct mention of someone who might not be comfortable with what you've written. You may have decided, as we have, to use composite characters, one person who represents several different people and when necessary, you've changed names and places. You realize the ultimate criteria for your Cycle Journey Story is whether it brings forward the feelings and emotions you've attached to the stages, not whether the scenes are a literal retelling of your journey.

C. G. Jung's Story

"There can be no transforming of darkness into light and of apathy into movement without emotions."

Jung's quotes as much as anything else we read, influenced us to write the Humpty Dumpty Principle. Carl Jung (1875 – 1961) the famous Swiss psychologist and founder of analytical psychology is best known for studies of the human psyche, dream analysis, the collective unconscious, active imagination, archetypes and individuation.

"We can discern, the sole purpose of human existence is to kindle a light in the darkness of mere being."

Jung was a practicing clinician and theoretical psychologist who explored widely diverse areas, including alchemy, astrology, the tarot, Eastern and Western philosophy, literature, the arts and sociology. He built his influence on unique communication skills centered on his logical thinking and mixing spirituality and the subconscious realms.

"No one can become aware of his individuality unless he is closely and responsibly related to his fellow beings."

Early in Jung's career he formed a friendship with Sigmund Freud, who had a major impact on Jung's later theories and helped him develop a fascination for the unconscious mind. Jung wanted to further his understanding of the human mind through dreams, myth, art and philosophy. Their friendship began to dissolve when Jung developed ideas which diverged from his mentor. He rejected Freud's emphasis on sex as the sole source of behavior motivation and became increasingly interested in dreams and symbols, later using what he learned as the basis for his theories of psychology.

**"The word "happiness" would lose its meaning
if it were not balanced by sadness."**

Jung realized his work could be applied to the interpretation of myths, folktales, religious symbols and art.

After suffering a brief illness, at age 86 Jung died at his home in Zurich on June 6th, 1961.

"Who looks outside, dreams; who looks inside awakes."

In the Humpty Dumpty Principle we've included Deeper Insights on Jungian topics impacting our Cycle Journey, including the Self and individuation, the unconscious and its shadow, and active imagination.

St. John of the Cross and the Dark Night

The Dark Night of the Soul, the emotional impact of a great fall, is the foundation of the Cycle Journey. The term came into being when at thirty-five years of age John of the Cross experienced a life changing event. From his tragic story comes the term Dark Night of the Soul.

John was born into a poor family in the small town of Fontiveros, Spain in 1542. John began to work in a hospital at a young age, caring for those plagued with syphilis. He met a Carmelite priest who sponsored him to study theology at the University of Salamanca and, to attend the University, he joined the Carmelite Order.

John became disillusioned with the Church dogma and considered leaving the order, before he met St. Teresa of Avila, who wanted to reform the Carmelites. She recognized his yearning for the simple life of contemplation. Since he was a devout Carmelite, she believed he could help her restore holy inspiration to the order.

Officials in Rome did not support the reform movement. In 1577, at age thirty-five, John suffered his great fall when he was captured and taken to Toledo to be questioned. There he was imprisoned in a dark closet and let out only to be continually tortured. During the winter he froze and in the summer the wilting heat rotted his clothes. In prison John began to wonder if he had been betrayed by his faith. To reclaim his faith, he composed passionate love poems to God, including *Songs of the Soul: One Dark Night*, which is a metaphor for the spiritual journey.

Mirabai Star's *Dark Night of the Soul: St John of the Cross* tells how, after his imprisonment, Saint John composed additional love poems to God and worked toward the Carmelite reformation. In later life, believing his soul needed to leave the everyday world, John spent his days in divine contemplation. When he was dying and John's fellow priests gathered around him, he whispered: "Into your hands, Beloved, I commend my spirit."

John's complete writings were not published until forty years after his death. Ninety-five years later, in 1675, Pope Benedict XIII canonized him. In the middle of the twentieth century, John was officially named a patron of Spanish poets. In the introduction to her translation Mirabai Starr concluded, "Even now, John is little known outside of Spain or beyond the confines of academic and theological studies. Many people toss around the term 'dark night of the soul' in reference to a period of personal pain arising from a bad divorce or a career catastrophe. Few people are familiar with John as the articulator of a brilliant and penetrating teaching on love and emptiness."

A Review of Literature

Seventeen Books That Support the Cycle Journey

Our book selections provide new insights and increased awareness for those taking the Cycle Journey. They cover a wide range of topics from acceptance and the hero's journey to the soul, symbols, and heartbreak. You'll find our comments at the end of each book description. Use the review to build your own library, read for greater depth on many of the topics covered in the Principle or simply enjoy the thoughtful ideas and concepts put forward by these authors.

1. Brach, Tara Ph.D., *Radical Acceptance, Embracing Your Life with the Heart of a Buddha* (2003). Dr. Brach proposes even if we believe something is wrong with us, we don't have to waste our lives carrying the belief. By using the process of Radical Acceptance we can free ourselves through training and meditation from the suffering and wounds life brings us. We are able to discover the pure awareness and love which are our deepest nature. Dr. Brach is a clinical psychologist, lecturer, workshop leader, and the founder and senior teacher of the Insight Meditation Community of Washington. She has practiced meditation since 1975 and leads Buddhist meditation retreats at centers throughout North America.
Sylvia's Notes: Radical Acceptance includes guided reflections and meditations. The meditation the Sacred Pause helps to reconnect with the present moment. Her book also helps in the acceptance stage where you need to move beyond the inner critic. I used the three guided meditations on Cultivating a Forgiving Heart: Asking for Forgiveness, Forgiving Ourselves, and Forgiving Others. For me forgiveness of myself and others were a necessary step before full acceptance could take place.

2. Campbell, Joseph. *The Hero's Journey: On His Life and Work* (1990). The greatest mythologist of the twentieth century was also a masterful storyteller. With poetry and humor, he recounts his own quest and conveys the excitement of his lifelong exploration of our mythic traditions, what he called "the one great story of mankind." Campbell is widely credited with bringing mythology to a mass audience. His works including *The Hero with a Thousand Faces*, the four-volume *The Masks of God* and *The Power of Myth* (with Bill Moyers), rank among the classics in mythology and literature.
    Court's Notes: Campbell defined the basic criteria for a Cycle Journey in his Hero's Journey, where a person goes through evolving stages and returns to where he or she started, changed forever.

3. Corbett, Lionel, M.D. *Psyche and the Sacred: Spirituality beyond Religion* (2007). Dr. Corbett's view of Spirituality is not tied to the Christian or other organized religions. His approach to spirituality is based on personal experience of the sacred. Using the language and insights of depth psychology, Corbett outlines the intimate relationship between spiritual experience and the psychology of the individual, unveiling the seamless continuity between the personal and transpersonal dimensions of the psyche. He shows there is a clear path to understanding the sacred language of the psyche and presents approaches to embrace the unknown. Lionel Corbett, M.D. teaches depth psychology at Pacifica Graduate Institute, in Santa Barbara, California. He is the author of *The Religious Function of the Psyche*, *The Sacred Cauldron*, and other books on Spirituality and the Psyche.
    Sylvia's Notes: Psyche & the Sacred and the six month class taught by Lionel gave me life- changing insights and grew my spiritual awareness. His view of what a spiritually-oriented life means is especially important for Self-discovery and spiritual growth. This is a must read book!

4. Frager, Robert Ph.D. and James Fadiman Ph.D. *Personality and Personal Growth, 6th Edition* (2005). The authors describe their book this way, "We present each student with a book that encourages and supports them as they evaluate each theory. Every chapter focuses on a theory's positive and useful aspects and reasons why it remains in wide use, rather than its limitations. We encourage students to test each theory's validity or utility against their own life experience and common sense." There are twelve theorists and three traditions explored in this carefully structured text book. Robert Frager received his Ph.D. in social psychology from Harvard University, where he was a teaching assistant to Erik Erikson. James Fadiman received his Ph.D. in psychology from Stanford University and has his own consulting firm offering seminars to executives and educators in the United States and abroad.

   Sylvia's Notes: Frager's text is the best overview of psychology I've read. It helped to broaden my perspective on how the different psychological theories influence our actions and reactions to life experiences.

5. Hale, Constance. *Sin and Syntax* (1999). The subtitle How to Craft *Wickedly* Effective Prose describes the reason you want Hale's book close to you when you begin writing your scenes. Here's one of the sentences from the introduction, "Sin and Syntax is about the skill that allows you, the writer, to harness such complexities, to create prose that thrills."

   Court's Notes: In Part 3, Music, where Hale covers voice, lyricism, melody and rhythm, you'll find new ways to make your scenes come alive. Read the section on voice a couple of times. It gets to the heart of what scene writing is about.

6. Hay, Louise. *You Can Heal Your Life* (1999). Louise Hay, internationally renowned author and lecturer, brings you the beautiful gift edition of her 1984 landmark bestseller. Her key message in this powerful work is: "If we are willing to do the mental work, almost anything can be healed." She explains

how limiting beliefs and ideas are often the cause of illness, and shows how you can change your thinking and improve the quality of your life!

Sylvia's Notes: This is the first Self-development book I read after a devastating divorce. I was looking for some way to heal my broken heart and recover from suffering and grief. I couldn't have chosen a better book to help me begin my healing journey.

7.   Hillman, James. *The Soul's Code: In Search of Character and Calling* (1997). His research supports an in depth understanding of his Acorn Theory. He proposed a unique, formed soul is within us from birth, shaping us as much as it is shaped and leading us to the inner calling which embraces what we came into the world to do and to be. James Hillman was a psychologist, scholar, international lecturer, and the author of some twenty books. A Jungian analyst and originator of post-Jungian "archetypal psychology," he held teaching positions at Yale University, Syracuse University, the University of Chicago, and the University of Dallas (where he cofounded the Dallas Institute for the Humanities and Culture).

Court's Notes: The late Hillman's use of the Greek *Damion* leading us toward a destiny uniquely ours and is one of the foundation concepts behind our Cycle Journey. The people he chose to use as examples are the key to what makes the Soul's Code come alive.

8.   Jung, Carl M.D. *Man and his Symbols*: Conceived and Edited by Carl G. Jung (1964). The Section devoted to the process of Individuation written by Dr. M. L. von Franz, introduces a pattern of psychic growth for individuals. Dr. Jung discusses the concept and structure of the unconscious and its symbolic expression in dreams, as well as a model of the total psyche. More than anyone else who has studied human behavior, Jung's thinking has led our modern world to view depth psychology as a natural process. Swiss psychologist, Carl Jung, devoted the closing months of his life to editing this book and writing

his own section, which he completed only ten days before his death in 1961. He was encouraged to write *Man and his Symbols* to explain his ideas to those who had no special knowledge of psychology.

Sylvia's Notes: C. G. Jung's explanation of the individuation process allowed me to trust the messages from my unconscious inner wisdom which arrive through insights, intuitions, hunches, dreams and meditation. His body of work has had the utmost influence in my self-discovery and personal transformation.

9. May, Gerald, M.D. *The Dark Night of the Soul: A Psychiatrist Explores the Connection between Darkness and Spiritual Growth* (2004). May's book focuses on how our darkest times are filled with a desperation necessary for spiritual growth. It provides both inspiration and hope that every Dark Night journey will bring an awakening into freedom and joy. He proposes after the awakening, the Dark Night brings precious gifts for the human soul. Gerald G. May, M.D., practiced medicine and psychiatry for twenty-five years before joining the full-time staff at the Shalem Institute for Spiritual Formation in Bethesda, Maryland, where he is a Senior Fellow in Contemplative Theology and Psychology. He is the author of books and articles on spirituality and psychology.

   Sylvia's Notes: He inspires and gives hope there is a purpose to the dark and challenging times we experience.

10. Moore, Thomas. *Dark Nights of the Soul: A Guide to Finding Your Way through Life's Ordeals* (2004). Moore tells us a Dark Night of the Soul is not extraordinary or rare and believes the Dark Night is a natural part of life which presents an opportunity to learn from its pain and confusion. He uses his insight into the dark times to get us to see them as friends and teachers rather than threats and discusses the difference between depression and a Dark Night. Thomas Moore is one of the most profound spiritual writers of our time. He has lived as a monk in a

Catholic religious order for twelve years and has degrees in theology, musicology, and philosophy.

Sylvia's Notes: This book introduced me to the Dark Night of the Soul. It explains a complex process in a simple and clear way. Moore tells how trauma is a natural part of life which provides a chance to learn what one needs to know for spiritual growth. I read this filled with grief after my mother's death and found it comforting.

11. Moore, Thomas. *Care of the Soul: A Guide for Cultivating Depth and Sacredness in Everyday Life* (1992). Moore observes understanding the soul can be deceptively simple. He believes you take back what has been disowned and work with what is, rather than with what you wish were there. Moore asks you to look at reality in a more expansive and imaginative way. He defines Soul as a quality or dimension of experiencing life. Its goal is not to make life problem-free, but to give ordinary life personal meaning. Thomas Moore is a lecturer and writer in North America and Europe in the areas of archetypal psychology, mythology and the imagination.

    Sylvia's Notes: Moore has the best explanation of Soul as a dimension of experiencing life and how soul gives ordinary life a deeper meaning.

12. Paris, Ginette Ph.D. *Heartbreak: New Approaches to Healing, Recovering from Lost Love and Mourning* (2011) Dr. Paris presents research about the impact on the brain from heartbreak from loss. She shows heartbreak is neurologically similar to being submitted to torture. Paris proposes recovery from loss involves processes called neurogenesis and individuation, in which the whole brain must re-configure its connections and its thinking about love and relationships. Dr. Paris is core faculty at the Pacifica Graduate Institute in Santa Barbara. She is the author, among other books, of Wisdom of the Psyche: Depth Psychology after Neuroscience (2007).

Sylvia's Notes: Her book brought tears to my eyes as I remembered two devastating heartbreaks and the emotional breakdowns tied to them. I realized those intense feelings meant I had to take heartbreak seriously. This is a must read book if you have suffered from a relationship heartbreak. Dr. Paris helped me focus on my recovery by giving me new awareness and understanding of the impact heartbreak and significant loss has on the brain and body.

13. Pearson, Carol S. Ph.D. *Awakening the Heroes Within: Twelve Archetypes to Help Us Find Ourselves and Transform Our World* (1991) Dr. Pearson presents a model for learning how to live by using stories of heroism. The Hero's Journey is first about taking a journey to find the treasure of your true Self. This book is written for people at all stages of the journey. She believes we are aided on our journey by inner guides or archetypes, each of which exemplifies a way of being and has a lesson to teach us. Carol S. Pearson Ph. D. was the President of Pacifica Graduate Institute in Santa Barbara, California. She is the bestselling author of The Hero Within.

    Sylvia's Notes: Dr. Pearson provides a view of a self-discovery journey which focuses on twelve archetypes to help us find ourselves. She includes a Heroic Myth questionnaire which aids in identifying your dominant archetype.

14. Ronnberg, Ami, and Kathleen Martin. *The Book of Symbols: Reflections on Archetypal Images.* (2010). The original essays in this volume are accompanied by art images from around the world and from every era where human beings used simple tools and objects to depict on rocks and cave walls psyche's imagined forms. These same forms appear in individual's dreams and fantasies. Together image and text open up a symbol and tell what its intrinsic qualities evoke and show how it mysteriously unites disparities. Drawing upon Jung's work on the archetype and the collective unconscious, the Archive for Research in Archetypal Symbolism (ARAS) is a pictorial and written

archive of mythological, ritualistic and symbolic images from all over the world and from all epochs of human experience.

Court's Notes: This volume goes into depth to tie symbols to their mythical and cultural origins. If you have an interest in learning how to understand and use symbols, you can't do any better than The Book of Symbols. You'll find the more you understand how to interpret and use symbols, the easier it will be for you to write greater depth into your scenes.

15. Salzberg, Sharon. *Real Happiness: The Power of Meditation.* (2011). Salzberg presents a twenty-eight-day plan for learning how to use meditation which helps defuse stress, experience greater tranquility, find a sense of wholeness and balance, strengthen relationships, and face fears. Meditation also sharpens focus, lowers blood pressure, and reduces chronic pain. It aids in protecting the brain against aging and improves the capacity for learning. Beginning with the simplest breathing and sitting techniques, Sharon distills thirty years of experience teaching, shows how to start and maintain an effective meditation practice with a commitment of twenty minutes a day. She explains how meditation has the potential to transform lives, is not religious, and can bring about a greater engagement with the world. The book includes a CD of four guided meditations. After reading the meditation, you can close your eyes and listen to Sharon guide you through the practice. Sharon Salzberg cofounded the Insight Meditation Society with Jack Kornfield and Joseph Goldstein, and is the author of eight books, including the bestselling *Loving Kindness and Faith.*

Sylvia's Notes: This is a must read book for learning about the power of meditation and how to simply integrate the practice into your life over a four week period. Meditation aids me in all areas of life. I am calmer, clearer thinking, and more aware of what is happening in the present moment. Instead of acting and re-acting based on past experience, I can choose how I want to react based on the present situation. Contemplative meditation is the core practice which supported my transformative journey.

16. Starr, Mirabai. *Dark Night of the Soul: St. John of the Cross* (2002) translated by Mirabai Starr offers an introduction to the life of John of the Cross and his torturous imprisonment where he experienced a crisis of faith. Starr tells how, after he escaped, in a state of ecstasy he wrote a poem entitled Songs of the Soul: One Dark Night, which is a metaphor for the spiritual journey. Later he wrote a commentary on his mystical verses which gave rise to the spiritual treatise known as Dark Night of the Soul. Starr is a writer of fiction and essays and an adjunct professor of philosophy, religious studies and Spanish at the University of New Mexico at Taos. She has studied St. John of the Cross's texts for more than twenty years.
    Sylvia's Notes: Saint John's story is where the term Dark Night or Dark Night of the Soul originated and where my study of the Dark Night Journey began. John's in-depth view on the soul's journey to the ultimate union with God reflects his passion and love for spiritual understanding.

17. Wilkinson, Kathryn. *Signs and Symbols: An Illustrated Guide to Their Origins and Meanings.* (2008). Kathryn Wilkinson is the Project Manager for this comprehensive book covering everything from simple shapes and colors to gods, mythical beasts, sacred rituals, and global branding. The Guide includes over 2,000 signs and symbols. Signs & Symbols explores the origins and meanings of the icons, markings, and pictures which have been used over the centuries and reveals how they have been interpreted in myth, religion, folklore, art, and contemporary culture. Explained through authoritative text and striking illustrations and photography, this indispensable guide brings a fresh understanding of the visual world.
    Court's Notes: This colorful book is a broad survey of signs and symbols taking you from the cosmos and the natural world through myths and religions and symbol systems. You'll find the expanded view of signs and symbols helps you recognize these objects and concepts in your own life and makes it easier to use them as metaphors, similes, analogies and even as a basis for poems.

Bibliography

Adams, Douglas. *The Long Dark Tea-Time of the Soul,* Penguin Books 1982.

Biography.com. *Frida Kahlo* 2014.

Black, Conrad. *Franklin Delano Roosevelt, Champion of Freedom*, Public Affairs 2005.

Brach, Tara Ph.D. *Radical Acceptance, Embracing Your Life with the Heart of a Buddha,* Bantam Books 2004.

Bronte, Charlotte. *Jane Eyre*, Barnes & Noble Classics 1993.

Campbell, Joseph. *The Hero's Journey: On His Life and Work,* New World Library 1990. 1947.

Campbell, Joseph. *The Hero With A thousand Faces*, Princeton University Press 1968.

Capra, Frank. *It's A Wonderful Life*, RKO Radio Pictures 1947, based on the short story *The Greatest Gift* by Philip Van Doren Smith.

Carroll, Lewis, illustrated by Blanche McManus. *Wonderland,* Mansfield & Wessels, 1899.

Cervantes, Miguel De. *Don Quixote*, Penguin Classics 2003.

Corbett, Lionel, M.D. *Psyche and the Sacred: Spirituality beyond Religion,* Spring Journal Inc. 2007.

Denslow W. W. *Denslow's Humpty Dumpty*, G. W. Dillingham 1903.

Evans, Nicholas. *The Horse Wisperer,* Dell reprint edition 2011.

Frager, Robert Ph.D. and James Fadiman Ph.D. *Personality and Personal Growth, 6th Edition,* Prentice Hall 2005.

Gardner, Marin. *The Annotated Alice Illustrated by John Tenniel*, Bramhall House 1960.

Guest, Judith. *Ordinary People* Penguin Books 1982.

Hale, Constance. *Sin and Syntax,* Three Rivers Press 1999.

Hillman, James. *The Soul's Code: In Search of Character and Calling,* Grand Central Publishing 1997.

Hooper, Tom. *The King's Speech*, Distributor The Weinstein Co., written by David Seidler 2010 Film.

Isaacson, Walter. *Steve Jobs*, Simon and Schuster 2011.

Jung, Carl M.D. *Man and his Symbols*: Conceived and Edited by Carl G. Jung, Dell Publishing 1968.

Knott, Steven. *Great Men In History, Gandhi*, Amazon Digital Services.

Malory, Sir Tomas,. *Le Morte D'Arthur*, Barnes and Noble Books 2004.

May, Gerald, M.D. *The Dark Night of the Soul: A Psychiatrist Explores the Connection between Darkness and Spiritual Growth*, Harper One reprint Edition 2004.

Mayes, Frances. *Under The Tuscan Sun*, Broadway Books reprint eidition 1997.

McGowan, Michael. *Saint Ralph*, Alliance Alantis 2004.

Melville, Herman, *Mobey Dick or The Whale*, Easton Press 1977

Meyers, Nancy. *Something's Gotta Give*, Columbia Pictures 2003 Film.

Meyers, Nancy. *It's Complicated*, Universal Pictures 2009 Film.

Miller, Frank and David Mazzucchelli. *Batman: Year One*, DC Comics DeLuxe Edition 2007.

Moore, Thomas. *Dark Nights of the Soul: A Guide to Finding Your Way through Life's Ordeals*, Gotham Books 2004.

Obdtfield, Raymond. *Crafting Scenes*, Writer's Digest Books 2000.

Paris, Ginette Ph.D. *Heartbreak: New Approaches to Healing, Recovering from Lost Love and Mourning*, Mill City Press 2011.

Parks, Rosa. *My Story*, Puffin Books reprint edition 1999.

Pearson, Carol S. Ph.D. *Awakening the Heroes Within: Twelve Archetypes to Help Us Find Ourselves and Transform Our World*, HarperElixir 1991.

Ronnberg, Ami, and Kathleen Martin. *The Book of Symbols: Reflections on Archetypal Images*, Taschen 2010.

Salzberg, Sharon. *Real Happiness: The Power of Meditation*, Workman Publishing Company 2011.

Selesisu, Angelus. *The Cherubinic Wanderer*, Hyperion Library of World Literature 1978.

Shakespeare, *William, Richard II act 4 sc. 1*, The Yale Shakespeare, Barnes and Noble Books 1993.

Shinner, William L. *Gandhi, A Memoir*, Simon and Schuster 1980.

Shaw, George Bernard. *Pygmalion*, Xist Classics, Kindle edition 2015.

Starr, Mirabai. *Dark Night of the Soul: St. John of the Cross*, translated by Mirabai Starr, Riverhead Books 2003.

Strayed, Cheryl, *Wild* Vintage 2013.

Tartt, Donna. *The Goldfinch*, Little Brown and Company 2013.

Tolkien, J. R. R. *The Lord Of The Rings*, Houghton Mifflin 1954.

Vogler, Christopher. *The Writer's Journey*, Michael Wise Productions 1998.

Wheelright, Jane Hollister and Lynda Wheelright Schmidt. *The Long Shore*, *A Psychological Experience of the Wilderness*, Sierra Club andNatural Philosophy Library 1991.

Wilkinson, Kathryn. *Signs and Symbols: An Illustrated Guide to Their Origins and Meanings*, Dorling Kindersley Limited 2008.

The Authors

Sylvia Stallings, Ph.D.

Sylvia is the originator of the Cycle Journey. Her conflict-filled relationships, heartbreak, and misfortune have given her an extra sensitivity and empathy for those who face upheaval, trauma and loss. Her main interest is sharing the hard-earned insights and inner wisdom of all that is involved in personal healing during a Cycle Journey. Sylvia's goal is to help those drawn into this spiritual rite-of-passage gain a perspective on what happened to them and how a Dark Night can provide an opportunity to discover one's true Self and life path.

Sylvia received her Ph.D. in Metaphysical Sciences from the University of Metaphysical Sciences, an international organization dedicated to assisting people in becoming knowledgeable about metaphysical concepts and discovering the true Self.

Court Johnson

Court is a writer and storyteller who specializes in creative non-fiction, mythic fantasy tales and using The Tell* Journal* Write Concept to tell ones personal story. He has expanded the uses of Active Imagination in creative non-fiction and storytelling, created the Cycle Journey Story format and developed scene writing for personal stories. He has made a study of mythic story formats and how they can be updated and used to illustrate psychological concepts such as the Dark Night. Court has a background in publishing and has taught communication skills in the newspaper and publishing industries.

The Cycle Journey Series Continues
Coming Winter 2016

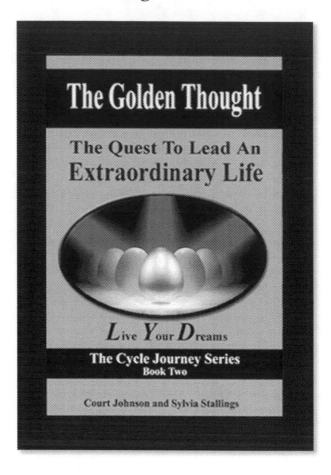

The Pursuit Of An Authentic Destiny

Whether you are in your twenties or thirties and looking to expand your future, at mid-life and and needing a new direction or mature enough to want to do more than retire, the quest is a change point that puts you in touch with your authentic destiny. In today's competitive world, undertaking a quest is a way to prove one's self and make dreams come true. Learn ancient questing skills and journey through the Eight Realms of Questing to reach the extraordinary promise your life offers.

Printed in the United States
By Bookmasters